Situation Ethics

E Raymond Walker
Clydebank '70.

SITUATION ETHICS

THE NEW MORALITY

by

Joseph Fletcher

SCM PRESS LTD
Bloomsbury Street London

To our children and grandchildren:
Joe, Jane, Bob, Maddy, Julia, Tommy

SBN 334 01538 3
First British edition 1966
Second impression 1969
© W. L. Jenkins 1966
Typeset in the United States of America
and printed in Great Britain by
Billing & Sons Ltd
Guildford and London

All moral laws, I wish to shew, are merely statements that certain kinds of actions will have good effects. The very opposite of this view has been generally prevalent in Ethics. "The right" and "the useful" have been supposed to be at least *capable* of conflicting with one another, and, at all events, to be essentially distinct. It has been characteristic of a certain school of moralists, as of moral common sense, to declare that the end will never justify the means. What I wish first to point out is that "right" does and can mean nothing but "cause of a good result," and is thus identical with "useful": whence it follows that the end always will justify the means, and that no action which is not justified by its results can be right.

—George Edward Moore,
Principia Ethica, p. 146.

The true, to put it briefly, is only the expedient in the way of our thinking, just as the right is only the expedient in the way of our behaving.

—William James, *Pragmatism*, p. 222.

The simple-minded use of the notions "right or wrong" is one of the chief obstacles to the progress of understanding.

—Alfred North Whitehead,
Modes of Thought, p. 15.

Such as transgress without a cause shall be put to confusion.
—Psalm 25:2, *The Book of Common Prayer.*

There is only one ultimate and invariable duty, and its formula is "Thou shalt love thy neighbour as thyself." How to do this is another question, but this is the whole of moral duty.
—William Temple, *Mens Creatrix,* p. 206.

The law of love is the ultimate law because it is the negation of law; it is absolute because it concerns everything concrete. . . . The absolutism of love is its power to go into the concrete situation, to discover what is demanded by the predicament of the concrete to which it turns. Therefore, love can never become fanatical in a fight for the absolute, or cynical under the impact of the relative.
—Paul Tillich,
Systematic Theology, Vol. I, p. 152.

Contents

Some British Editions of Books Mentioned in the Text

Anderson, R., *Tea and Sympathy* (Heinemann, 1956).

Berdyaev, N., *The Destiny of Man* (Bles, 1937).

Bernard, St, *On the Love of God*, newly translated by a Religious of CSMV (Mowbray, 1956).

Bonhoeffer, D., *Ethics* (SCM Press, 1955; Collins, 1964).
Letters and Papers from Prison (SCM Press, 1956; Fontana, 1959).

Bornkamm, G., *Jesus of Nazareth* (Hodder, 1960).

Bruckberger, R., *Image of America* (Longmans, 1960).

Brunner, E., *The Divine Imperative* (Lutterworth Press, 1946).
Faith, Hope and Love (Lutterworth Press, 1957).

Bultmann, R., *Essays Philosophical and Theological* (SCM Press, 1955).
Jesus and the Word (Collins, 1962).

Burnaby, J. (ed.) *Augustine: Later Works*, Library of Christian Classics, Vol. VIII (SCM Press, 1955).

Cahn, E., *The Moral Decision* (Stevens & Sons, 1959).

D'Arcy, M. C., *The Mind and Heart of Love* (Faber, 1945; Fontana, 1963).

Dewey, J., *The Quest of Certainty* (Allen & Unwin, 1929).
(with J. N. Tufts), *Ethics* (Bell, 1908).

Dodd, C. H., *Gospel and Law* (Cambridge, 1951).

Driberg, T., *The Mystery of Moral Rearmament* (Secker & Warburg, 1964).

Duff, E., *The Social Thought of the World Council of Churches* (Longmans, 1956).

Ewing, A. C., *The Definition of the Good* (Routledge, 1947).

Friedman, M., *Martin Buber: The Life of Dialogue* (Routledge, 1955).

Fromm, E., *Man for Himself: An Inquiry into the Psychology of Ethics* (Routledge, 1949).

Häring, B., *The Law of Christ*, 2 vols. (Mercier Press, 1962-3).

Heidegger, M., *Being and Time* (SCM Press, 1962).

Hospers, J., *Human Conduct* (Hart-Davis, 1961).

Kierkegaard, S., *The Works of Love* (Oxford, 1946).

Lehmann, P., *Ethics in a Christian Context* (SCM Press, 1963).

Lewis, C. S., *The Four Loves* (Bles, 1960; Fontana, 1963).

McIntyre, J., *On the Love of God* (Collins, 1962).

Miller, A., *The Renewal of Man* (Gollancz, 1956).

Niebuhr, H. R., *Christ and Culture* (Faber, 1952).

Niebuhr, Reinhold, *An Interpretation of Christian Ethics* (SCM Press, 1935).

Moral Man and Immoral Society (SCM Press, 1963).

The Nature and Destiny of Man, 2 vols. (Nisbet, 1941-3).

Nygren, A., *Agape and Eros* (SPCK, 1953).

Pierce, C. A., *Conscience in the New Testament* (SCM Press, 1955).

Quick, O. C., *The Doctrines of the Creed* (Nisbet, 1938; Fontana, 1963).

Ramsey, P., *Basic Christian Ethics* (SCM Press, 1953).

Rand, A., *Atlas Shrugged* (Muller, 1957).

Rapoport, A., *Fights, Games and Debates* (Cresset Press, 1960).

Robinson, J. A. T., *Christian Morals Today* (SCM Press, 1964).

Honest to God (SCM Press, 1963).

Sartre, J.-P., *Being and Nothingness* (Methuen, 1957).

Tillich, P., *Morality and Beyond* (Routledge, 1964).

Systematic Theology, 3 vols. (Nisbet, 1941-3, 1963).

Vidler, A. R., *The Theology of F. D. Maurice* (American title: *Witness to the Light*) (SCM Press, 1948).

Foreword

AT HARVARD UNIVERSITY some years ago, e. e. cummings gave his six *nonlectures*[1] on poetry, which some of his critics call "six lectures on nonpoetry." The poet's experience speaks to my condition. Over the years, as I have lectured on non-Christian systems of ethics, comparing them to various Christian systems, I have sometimes included my own *non*system. It is this "nonsystem" which is set forth in capsule form in these pages.

In some cases my critics, like cummings', have argued that my point of view actually represents a Christian system of nonethics. A few have treated it as a non-Christian system of nonethics; and one moral theologian in Ireland has, in effect, taken it to be a non-Christian nonsystem of nonethics![2] On the other hand, Bishop Robinson, discussing "the new morality" in his *Honest to God*,[3] is amiable enough to say that my analysis gives it (the new morality) the "most consistent" statement he knows. We shall see.

The reader will find a method here, but no system. It is a method of "situational" or "contextual" decision-making, but system-building has no part in it. I gladly echo

[1] *Six nonlectures* (Harvard University Press, 1953).

[2] C. B. Daly, "A Criminal Lawyer on the Sanctity of Life," *Irish Theological Quarterly,* Vol. XXV (1958), pp. 330–366; Vol. XXVI (1959), pp. 23–55, 231–272.

[3] The Westminster Press, 1963.

F. D. Maurice on "system" and "method." He found them
"not only not synonymous, but the greatest contraries
imaginable: the one indicating that which is most opposed
to life, freedom, variety; and the other that without which
they cannot exist."[4] If this is "system-phobia," let the
epithet be duly noted! Bishop Robinson rightly says that
"there is no one ethical system that can claim to be Christian,"[5] but I am inclined to say that *any* ethical system
is unchristian or at least sub-Christian, whatever might
be its claim to theological orthodoxy.

Bultmann was correct in saying that Jesus had no
ethics, if we accept, as I do not, his definition of ethics
as a *system* of values and rules "intelligible for all men."[6]
Yet the point is not so much that there *is* no such universal
ethic (on that score Bultmann is on entirely firm ground)
but that no ethic *need* be systematic and Jesus' ethic most
certainly *was* not! I accept Hendrik Kraemer's trenchant
statement: "Christian living . . . can never be stabilized
in any historical or theoretical system, the splendid theo-
retic laws of the Old Testament included. There may be
systems of philosophical ethics; there can never be a
system of Christian ethics, at least if it is true to its
nature."[7]

The label "new morality" is not altogether justified. Its
meaning in journalism is a relaxed or even lax ethical
outlook, especially in matters sexual. Two things should
become clear as we proceed: (1) that the "new morality"

[4] Quoted in A. R. Vidler, *Witness to the Light* (Charles
Scribner's Sons, 1948), p. 13.

[5] John A. T. Robinson, *Christian Morals Today* (The
Westminster Press, 1964), p. 18.

[6] Rudolf Bultmann, *Jesus and the Word,* tr. by Louise Petti-
bone Smith and Erminie Huntress Lantero (Charles Scribner's Sons, 1958), p. 84.

[7] Quoted in Edward Duff, S.J., *The Social Thought of the
World Council of Churches* (Association Press, 1956), p.
103n.

is not exactly new, either in method or in content, and (2) that as a method (which is the primary focus of this essay) its *roots* lie securely, even if not conventionally, in the classical tradition of Western Christian morals. It's an old posture with a new and contemporary look. At the same time, to be candid, the new morality—i.e., situation ethics—is a radical departure from the conventional wisdom and prevailing climate of opinion. In the language fashionable just now, the problem solver and the decision maker will see that situation ethics is not particularly Catholic or Protestant or Orthodox or humanist. It extricates us from the *odium theologicum*.

Let an anecdote set the tone. A friend of mine arrived in St. Louis just as a presidential campaign was ending, and the cab driver, not being above the battle, volunteered his testimony. "I and my father and grandfather before me, and their fathers, have always been straight-ticket Republicans." "Ah," said my friend, who is himself a Republican, "I take it that means you will vote for Senator So-and-So." "No," said the driver, "there are times when a man has to push his principles aside and do the right thing." That St. Louis cabbie is this book's hero.

Look also at a passage in Nash's play *The Rainmaker*. On the stage and as a movie it was a great success. But the key to it, ethically, lies in a scene where the morally outraged brother of a lonely, spinsterized girl threatens to shoot the sympathetic but not "serious" Rainmaker because he makes love to her in the barn at midnight. The Rainmaker's intention is to restore her sense of womanliness and her hopes for marriage and children. Her father, a wise old rancher, grabs the pistol away from his son, saying, "Noah, you're so full of what's right you can't see what's good."[8] I nominate the Texas rancher as co-hero

[8] N. Richard Nash, *The Rainmaker* (Bantam Books, Inc., 1957), p. 99. See also Robert Anderson's *Tea and Sympathy* (The New American Library of World Literature, Inc., 1956), esp. Act III.

with the cab driver. (An English movie in the same genre is *The Mark,* in which a man is sexually attracted to little girls until a woman his own age rescues him by seducing him and releasing him from his pathology.[9] At least it worked in the movie!)

As Paul Ramsey has pointed out, with some distaste, my approach is both personalistic and contextual.[10] These seem to me to be the two main features of Christian situationism. But I should make clear at the outset what is meant by "contextual" in this book. Paul Lehmann muddies the water with his use of the term because he attaches to it two different but often confused meanings. Sometimes he means that Christian action is to be carried out within a theological frame of reference, in the *koinōnia,* in the context of *faith.* Sometimes he means that Christian action should be tailored to fit objective circumstances, the *situation.*[11] It is in this second sense that I use it. (After all, *all* Christian ethics is "contextual" in the first sense, but that deprives the term of any discrete meaning in theological ethics!) Properly used, the word is applicable to *any* situation-sensitive decision-making, whether its ideology is theological or nontheological—e.g., either Christian or Marxist.[12]

People in churches and students in the "religious" departments of universities (but not others) sometimes

[9] Cited by H. A. Williams, "Theology and Self-Awareness," in A. R. Vidler, ed., *Soundings: Essays in Christian Understanding* (Cambridge: Cambridge University Press, 1962), p. 82.

[10] "Lehmann's Contextual Ethics and the Problem of Truth-Telling," *Theology Today,* Vol. XXI (1965), p. 474.

[11] *Ethics in a Christian Context* (Harper & Row, Publishers, Inc., 1963).

[12] See a penetrating paper by James A. Gustafson, "Context Versus Principle: A Misplaced Debate in Christian Ethics," *Harvard Theological Review,* Vol. 58 (1965), pp. 171–202.

complain that I fail to treat situation ethics in a very "Christian way," meaning that I do not seem, at least explicitly and persistently, to make enough reference to the theological framework. This is often wittingly the case, except for a stress on the normative ideal of "love"— always carefully distinguished as New Testament *agapē*. My reason is that the basic challenge offered by the situationist has nothing to do in any special way with theological over against nontheological faith commitments —as we shall see. (This is not to say, however, that one's faith is without an important bearing upon the situationist's action and decision-making.)

One explanation should be made. The word "love" is a swampy one, a semantic confusion. Compare these statements: (1) "See it now! Uncensored! Love in the raw!" (2) "I just love that hat. Isn't it absolutely divine?" (3) "Do you promise to love, honor, and obey?" (4) "Aw, come on—just this once—prove your love." (5) "I love strawberries, but they give me a rash." (6) "So faith, hope, love abide, these three; but the greatest of these is love." (7) "And Jonathan loved David."

The temptation is to drop the word "love" altogether in Christian ethical discourse, to use only the New Testament word *agapē* (as Tillich has proposed[13]), or to hyphenate it with a C for Christian (C-love), or something of the kind. I appreciate the difficulty in using the simple English word (the Japanese have to cope with the same problem of multiple meanings in *ai*), but in this book I have kept it—with some explanation. The word is too rich, with too much important and legitimate meaning over and beyond its technical meaning in New Testament theology, to throw it away ruthlessly. Although not at all satisfied with his results, I am somehow impressed with the wealth of content in C. S. Lewis' *The Four Loves*.[14]

[13] *Morality and Beyond* (Harper & Row, Publishers, Inc., 1963), p. 39.

[14] London: Geoffrey Bles, Ltd., Publishers, 1960.

I am grateful for invitations to three lectureships which have helped me to crystallize this material. It began with the Alumni Visitation Day Lecture at the Harvard Divinity School in 1959; found fuller statement in the Easter Bedell Lectures at Bexley Hall, Kenyon College, in 1963; and won still further fashioning in the Visiting Professorship at International Christian University in Tokyo, 1963–1964. Throughout the preparation of these lectures and this book I have, as in past volumes, had the vital help and tolerance of my wife. And to students and practitioners in theological, medical, and business schools in various American universities I owe a lot for their illuminating discussions of both the theory itself and some real cases used to test it.

My greatest regret is that I did not have Professor Ramsey's quite remarkable symposium *Christian Ethics and Contemporary Philosophy* when this was written. He was thoughtful enough to send it to me in page proof but that was too late to cite or quote it. Nearly every paper in it is of the first importance and value to those who want to assess the merits of situation ethics, the ones by Dewi Phillips, of Bangor, and George Wood, of London, being quite directly relevant. Crossing swords with Ramsey's own concluding essay, about trying to find some way to rehabilitate the natural law theory, will have to wait upon later work.

JOSEPH FLETCHER

Cambridge, Massachusetts

I

Three Approaches

THERE ARE at bottom only three alternative routes or approaches to follow in making moral decisions. They are: (1) the legalistic; (2) the antinomian, the opposite extreme—i.e., a lawless or unprincipled approach; and (3) the situational. All three have played their part in the history of Western morals, legalism being by far the most common and persistent. Just as legalism triumphed among the Jews after the exile, so, in spite of Jesus' and Paul's revolt against it, it has managed to dominate Christianity constantly from very early days. As we shall be seeing, in many real-life situations legalism demonstrates what Henry Miller, in a shrewd phrase, calls "the immorality of morality."[1]

There is an old joke which serves our purposes. A rich man asked a lovely young woman if she would sleep the night with him. She said, "No." He then asked if she would do it for $100,000? She said, "Yes!" He then asked, "$10,000?" She replied, "Well, yes, I would." His next question was, "How about $500?" Her indignant "What do you think I am?" was met by the answer, "We have already established *that*. Now we are haggling over the price." Does any girl who has "relations" (what a funny way to use the word) outside marriage automatically be-

[1] *Stand Still Like the Hummingbird* (New Directions, 1962), pp. 92–96.

come a prostitute? Is it always, regardless of what she accomplishes for herself or others—is it *always* wrong? Is extramarital sex inherently evil, or can it be a good thing in some situations? Does everybody have his price, and if so, does that mean we are immoral and ethically weak? Let's see if we can find some help in answering these questions.

APPROACHES TO DECISION-MAKING

1. *Legalism*

With this approach one enters into every decision-making situation encumbered with a whole apparatus of prefabricated rules and regulations. Not just the spirit but the letter of the law reigns. Its principles, codified in rules, are not merely guidelines or maxims to illuminate the situation; they are *directives* to be followed. Solutions are preset, and you can "look them up" in a book—a Bible or a confessor's manual.

Judaism, Catholicism, Protestantism—all major Western religious traditions have been legalistic. In morals as in doctrine they have kept to a spelled-out, "systematic" orthodoxy. The ancient Jews, especially under the post-exilic Maccabean and Pharisaic leadership, lived by the law or Torah, and its oral tradition (halakah).[2] It was a code of 613 (or 621) precepts, amplified by an increasingly complicated mass of Mishnaic interpretations and applications.

Statutory and code law inevitably piles up, ruling upon ruling, because the complications of life and the claims of mercy and compassion combine—even with code legalists —to accumulate an elaborate system of exceptions and compromise, in the form of rules for breaking the rules! It leads to that tricky and tortuous now-you-see-it, now-

[2] The prophetic J tradition gave way to the E-D tradition, with its precepts and laws.

you-don't business of interpretation that the rabbis called pilpul—a hairsplitting and logic-chopping study of the letter of the law, pyramiding from codes (e.g., the Covenant and Holiness) to Pentateuch to Midrash and Mishna to Talmud. It was a tragic death to the prophets' "pathos" (sharing God's loving concern) and "ethos" (living by love as *norm*, not program). With the prophets it had been a question of sensitively seeking "an understanding of *the situation*."[3]

Any web thus woven sooner or later chokes its weavers. Reformed and even Conservative Jews have been driven to disentangle themselves from it. Only Orthodoxy is still in its coils. Something of the same pilpul and formalistic complication may be seen in Christian history. With Catholics it has taken the form of a fairly ingenious moral theology that, as its twists and involutions have increased, resorts more and more to a casuistry that appears (as, to its credit, it does) to evade the very "laws" of right and wrong laid down in its textbooks and manuals. Love, even with the most stiff-necked of system builders, continues to plead mercy's cause and to win at least partial release from law's cold abstractions. Casuistry is the homage paid by legalism to the love of persons, and to realism about life's relativities.

Protestantism has rarely constructed such intricate codes and systems of law, but what it has gained by its simplicity it has lost through its rigidity, its puritanical insistence on moral rules.[4] In fact, the very lack of a casuistry and its complexity, once people are committed to *even the bare principle* of legalistic morality or law ethics, is itself evidence of their blindness to the factors

[3] Abraham J. Heschel, *The Prophets* (Harper & Row, Publishers, Inc., 1962), pp. 225, 307–315.

[4] There are, however, atypical works such as Richard Baxter, *Christian Directory* (1673), and William Ames (Amesius), *De conscientia, eius jure et Casibus* (1632).

of doubt and perplexity. They have lost touch with the headaches and heartbreaks of life.

What can be worse, no casuistry at all may reveal a punishing and sadistic use of law to hurt people instead of helping them. How else explain burning at the stake in the Middle Ages for homosexuals (death, in the Old Testament)? Even today imprisonment up to sixty years is the penalty in one state for those who were actually consenting adults, without seduction or public disorder! This is really unavoidable whenever law instead of love is put first. The "puritan" type is a well-known example of it. But even if the legalist is truly *sorry* that the law requires unloving or disastrous decisions, he still cries, *"Fiat justitia, ruat caelum!"* (Do the "right" even if the sky falls down). He is the man Mark Twain called "a good man in the worst sense of the word."

The Christian situation ethicist agrees with Bertrand Russell and his implied judgment, "To this day Christians think an adulterer more wicked than a politician who takes bribes, although the latter probably does a thousand times as much harm."[5] And he thoroughly rejects Cardinal Newman's view: "The Church holds that it were better for sun and moon to drop from heaven, for the earth to fail, and for all the many millions who are upon it to die of starvation in extremest agony . . . than that one soul, I will not say should be lost, but should commit one single venial sin."[6]

A Mrs. X was convicted (later cleared in appellate court) of impairing the morals of her minor daughter. She had tried to teach the child chastity but at thirteen the girl bore the first of three unwanted, neglected babies. Her mother then had said, "If you persist in acting this

[5] *Why I Am Not a Christian* (Simon and Schuster, Inc., 1957), p. 33.

[6] J. H. Newman, *Certain Difficulties Felt by Anglicans in Catholic Teaching* (Longmans, Green & Co., Inc., 1918), p. 190.

way, at least be sure the boy wears something!" On this evidence she was convicted and sentenced. The combined forces of "secular" law and legalistic puritanism had tried to prevent loving help to the girl, her bastard victims, and the social agencies trying to help her. Situation ethics would have praised that woman; it would not have pilloried her.

In the language of classical ethics and jurisprudence, the more statutory the law, the greater the need of equity. For, as statutes are applied to actual situations, something has to give; some latitude is necessary for doubtful or perplexed consciences. Inexorably questions arise as to whether in a particular case the law truly applies (doubt), or as to which of several more or less conflicting laws is to be followed (perplexity). The effort to deal with these questions helpfully, even though hamstrung and corseted by rules and "sacred" principles, is what casuistry is. When a law ethic listens to love at all, it tries to rise above its legalism; paradoxically enough, the development of Catholic casuistry is powerful evidence of less legalism in the Catholic fold than the Protestant.

Legalism in the Christian tradition has taken two forms. In the Catholic line it has been a matter of legalistic *reason*, based on nature or natural law. These moralists have tended to adumbrate their ethical rules by applying human reason to the facts of nature, both human and subhuman, and to the lessons of historical experience. By this procedure they claim to have adduced universally agreed and therefore valid "natural" moral laws. Protestant moralists have followed the same adductive and deductive tactics. They have taken Scripture and done with it what the Catholics do with nature. Their Scriptural moral law is, they argue, based on the words and sayings of the Law and the Prophets, the evangelists and apostles of the Bible. It is a matter of legalistic *revelation*. One is rationalistic, the other Biblicistic; one natural, the other Scriptural. But both are legalistic.

Even though Catholic moralists deal also with "revealed law" (e.g., "the divine positive law of the Ten Commandments") and Protestants have tried to use reason in interpreting the sayings of the Bible (hermeneutics), still both by and large have been committed to the doctrines of law ethics.

2. *Antinomianism*

Over against legalism, as a sort of polar opposite, we can put antinomianism. This is the approach with which one enters into the decision-making situation armed with no principles or maxims whatsoever, to say nothing of *rules.* In every "existential moment" or "unique" situation, it declares, one must rely upon the situation of itself, *there and then,* to provide its ethical solution.

The term "antinomianism" (literally, "against law") was used first by Luther to describe Johannes Agricola's views. The ethical concept has cropped up here and there, as among some Anabaptists, some sects of English Puritanism, and some of Wesley's followers. The concept is certainly at issue in I Corinthians (e.g., ch. 6:12–20). Paul had to struggle with two primitive forms of it among the Hellenistic Jew-Christians whom he visited. They took his attacks on law morality too naïvely and too literally.

One form was libertinism—the belief that by grace, by the new life in Christ and salvation by faith, law or rules no longer applied to Christians. Their ultimate happy fate was now assured, and it mattered no more *what* they did. (Whoring, incest, drunkenness, and the like are what they did, therefore! This explains the warning in I Peter 2:16, "Live as free men, yet without using your freedom as a pretext for evil; but live as servants of God." This license led by inevitable reaction to an increase of legalism, especially in sex ethics, under which Christians still suffer today.) The other form, less pretentious and more enduring, was a Gnostic claim to special knowledge, so that neither principles nor rules were needed any longer even as guidelines and direction pointers. They would just *know* what was right when they needed to know. They had, they claimed, a superconscience. It is this second "gnostic" form of the approach which is under examination here.

While legalists are preoccupied with law and its stipulations, the Gnostics are so flatly opposed to law—even in principle—that their moral decisions are random, unpredictable, erratic, quite anomalous. Making moral decisions is a matter of spontaneity; it is literally unprincipled, purely *ad hoc* and casual. They follow no forecastable course from one situation to another. They are, exactly, anarchic—i.e., without a rule. They are not only "unbound by the chains of law" but actually sheer extemporizers, impromptu and intellectually irresponsible. They not only cast the old Torah aside; they even cease to think seriously and *care-fully* about the demands of love as it has been shown in Christ, the love norm itself. The baby goes out with the bath water!

This was the issue Paul fought over with the antinomians at Corinth and Ephesus. They were repudiating all law, as such, and all principles, relying in all moral action choices solely upon guidance in the situation. Some were what he called *pneumatikoi,* spirit-possessed. They claimed that *their* guidance came from outside themselves, by the Holy Spirit. Of what use are principles and laws when you can depend on the Holy Spirit? It was a kind of special-providence idea; a version of the inspiration theory of conscience.[7] Other antinomians claimed, and still do, that their guidance comes from within themselves, as a sort of built-in radarlike "faculty," a translegal or clairvoyant conscience as promised in Jer. 31:31–34, written "upon their hearts." This second and more common form of Gnostic antinomianism, found among both

[7] See warnings in Eph. 6:12; I Tim. 4:1.

Christians and non-Christians, is close to the intuition
theory or faculty theory of conscience.[8]

Perhaps a good example of the guidance idea in today's
scene is Moral Re-Armament. It has a doctrine of special
providence and daily guidance by "spiritual power" to
right and wrong actions and causes. Its basic doctrines
were first worked out under the leadership of Frank
Buchman in the twenties, when it was called "The First
Century Christian Fellowship." It has won to itself, not
so surprisingly, even the French Catholic existentialist
philosopher, Gabriel Marcel.[9]

In its present form, with its wealthy clientele, it is a
"sawdust trail in a dinner jacket." Part of its ideology,
understandably, is the perfectionist notion that "members
of the fellowship" can achieve and should live by *absolute*
purity (sexual!), *absolute* truth, *absolute* unselfishness,
and *absolute* love. Its separation of love from unselfishness
is as puzzling as its call for "absolute" virtue and perfectionism and is as pretentious. But after all, if we have the
power of the Spirit to tell us daily in a special way *what*
the good is, surely we can expect to *do* it "absolutely"!
Curiously, the Moral Re-Armament ethic is of the kind
one would logically expect to find in the Holiness and
Pentecostal movements, and yet, in spite of their self-
styled pneumatic character, they are for the most part
quite legalistic morally—not antinomian about their ethics
at all.

Another version of antinomianism, on the whole much
subtler philosophically and perhaps more admirable, is the
ethics of existentialism. Sartre speaks of "nausea," which
is our anxious experience of the *incoherence* of reality.
For him any belief in coherence (such as the Christian

[8] See note 22, Chapter II.
[9] Cf. Gabriel Marcel, *Fresh Hope for the World* (Longmans, Green & Co., Inc., 1960); see also Tom Driberg, *The
Mystery of Moral Re-Armament* (Alfred A. Knopf, Inc.,
1965).

doctrine of the unity of God's creation and his Lordship over history) is "bad faith." In every moment of moral choice or decision "we have no excuses behind us and no justification before us." Sartre refuses to admit to any *generally* valid principles at all, nothing even ordinarily valid, to say nothing of universal *laws*.[10] Simone de Beauvoir in *The Ethics of Ambiguity* cannot quite bring herself to accept either "the contingent absurdity of the discontinuous" or "the rationalistic necessity of the continuous," proving herself to be less sturdily existentialist than Sartre, but she admits that the real world is after all "bare and incoherent."[11] She shrinks from a candid antinomianism. But the plain fact is that her ontology—her idea of basic reality—is, like Sartre's, one of radical discontinuity, so that there can be no connective tissue between one situation or moment of experience and another. There is no fabric or web of life, hence no basis for generalizing moral principles *or* laws. Every situation has only its particularity!

On this view, of course, the existentialists rightly reject even all principles, all "generally valid" ethical norms or axioms, as well as all rules or laws or precepts that legalistically absolutize (idolize) such general principles. Radical discontinuity in one's theory of being forces the "absolute particularity" of *tout comprendre, tout pardonner.* Sartre is at least honest and tough-minded. In the absence of any faith in love as the norm and in any God as the norm-giver, he says resolutely: "Ontology itself cannot formulate ethical precepts. It is concerned solely with what is, and we cannot possibly derive imperatives from ontology's indicatives."[12] He is, on this score at least, entirely correct!

[10] Jean-Paul Sartre, *Existentialism,* tr. by B. Frechtman (Philosophical Library, Inc., 1947), p. 27.

[11] (Philosophical Library, Inc., 1948), pp. 44, 122.

[12] *Being and Nothingness,* tr. by Hazel Barnes (Philosophical Library, Inc., 1956), p. 625.

3. *Situationism*

A third approach, in between legalism and antinomian unprincipledness, is situation ethics. (To jump from one polarity to the other would be only to go from the frying pan to the fire.) The situationist enters into every decision-making situation fully armed with the ethical maxims of his community and its heritage, and he treats them with respect as illuminators of his problems. Just the same he is prepared in any situation to compromise them or set them aside *in the situation* if love seems better served by doing so.

Situation ethics goes part of the way with natural law, by accepting reason as the instrument of moral judgment, while rejecting the notion that the good is "given" in the nature of things, objectively. It goes part of the way with Scriptural law by accepting revelation as the source of the norm while rejecting all "revealed" norms or laws but the one command—to love God in the neighbor. The situationist follows a moral law or violates it according to love's need. For example, "Almsgiving is a good thing *if . . .*" The situationist never says, "Almsgiving is a good thing. Period!" His decisions are hypothetical, not categorical. Only the commandment to love is categorically good. "Owe no one anything, except to love one another." (Rom. 13:8.) If help to an indigent only pauperizes and degrades him, the situationist refuses a handout and finds some other way. He makes no law out of Jesus' "Give to every one who begs from you." It is only one step from that kind of Biblicist literalism to the kind that causes women in certain sects to refuse blood transfusions even if death results—even if they are carrying a quickened fetus that will be lost too. The legalist says that even if he tells a man escaped from an asylum where his intended victim is, if he finds and murders him, at least only one sin has been committed (murder), not two (lying as well)!

As Brunner puts it, "The basis of the Divine Command is always the same, but its content varies with varying circumstances." Therefore, the "error of casuistry does not lie in the fact that it indicates the infinite variety of forms which the Command of love may assume; its error consists in deducing particular laws from a universal law . . . as though all could be arranged beforehand. . . . Love, however, is free from all this predefinition."[13] We might say, from the situationist's perspective, that it is possible to derive general "principles" from whatever is the one and only universal law (*agapē* for Christians, something else for others), but not laws or rules. We cannot milk universals from a universal!

William Temple put it this way: "Universal obligation attaches not to particular judgments of conscience but to conscientiousness. What acts are right may depend on circumstances . . . but there is an absolute obligation to will whatever may on each occasion be right."[14] Our obligation is relative *to* the situation, but obligation *in* the situation is absolute. We are only "obliged" to tell the truth, for example, if the situation calls for it; if a murderer asks us his victim's whereabouts, our duty might be to lie. There is in situation ethics an absolute element and an element of calculation, as Alexander Miller once pointed out.[15] But it would be better to say it has an absolute *norm* and a calculating method. There is weight in the old saying that what is needed is "faith, hope, and clarity." We have to find out what is "fitting" to be truly ethical, to use H. R. Niebuhr's word for it in his *The Responsible Self*.[16] Situation ethics aims at a contextual

[13] *The Divine Imperative,* tr. by Olive Wyon (The Westminster Press, 1947), pp. 132 ff.

[14] *Nature, Man and God* (The Macmillan Company, 1934), p. 405.

[15] *The Renewal of Man* (Doubleday & Company, Inc., 1955), p. 44.

[16] (Harper & Row, Publishers, Inc., 1963), pp. 60 61.

appropriateness—not the "good" or the "right" but the *fitting*.

A cartoon in a fundamentalist magazine once showed Moses scowling, holding his stone tablet with its graven laws, all ten, and an eager stonecutter saying to him, "Aaron said perhaps you'd let us reduce them to 'Act responsibly in love.' " This was meant as a dig at the situationists and the new morality, but the legalist humor in it merely states exactly what situation ethics calls for! With Dietrich Bonhoeffer we say, "Principles are only tools in God's hands, soon to be thrown away as unserviceable."[17]

One competent situationist, speaking to students, explained the position this way. Rules are "like 'Punt on fourth down,' or 'Take a pitch when the count is three balls.' These rules are part of the wise player's know-how, and distinguish him from the novice. But they are not unbreakable. The best players are those who know when to ignore them. In the game of bridge, for example, there is a useful rule which says 'Second hand low.' But have you ever played with anyone who followed the rule slavishly? You say to him (in exasperation), 'Partner, why didn't you play your ace? We could have set the hand.' And he replies, unperturbed, 'Second hand low!' What is wrong? The same thing that was wrong when Kant gave information to the murderer. He forgot the purpose of the game. . . . He no longer thought of winning the hand, but of being able to justify himself by invoking the rule."[18]

This practical temper of the activist or *verb*-minded decision maker, versus contemplative *noun*-mindedness,

Precedents are Samuel Clarke, *Unchangeable Obligations of Natural Religion* (London, 1706), and A. C. Ewing, *The Definition of the Good* (The Macmillan Company, 1947).

[17] *Ethics,* tr. by N. H. Smith (The Macmillan Company, 1955), p. 8.

[18] E. LaB. Cherbonnier, unpublished address, Trinity College, December 14, 1964.

is a major Biblical rather than Hellenistic trait. In Abraham Heschel's view, "The insistence upon generalization at the price of a total disregard of the particular and concrete is something which would be alien to prophetic thinking. Prophetic words are never detached from the concrete, historic situation. Theirs is not a timeless, abstract message; it always refers to an actual situation. The general is given in the particular and the verification of the abstract is in the concrete."[19] A "leap of faith" is an action decision rather than a leap of thought, for a man's faith is a hypothesis that he takes seriously enough to act on and live by.

There are various names for this approach: situationism, contextualism, occasionalism, circumstantialism, even actualism. These labels indicate, of course, that the core of the ethic they describe is a healthy and primary awareness that "circumstances alter cases"—i.e., that in actual problems of conscience the situational variables are to be weighed as heavily as the normative or "general" constants.

The situational factors are so primary that we may even say "circumstances alter rules and principles." It is said that when Gertrude Stein lay dying she declared, "It is better to ask questions than to give answers, even good answers." This is the temper of situation ethics. It is empirical, fact-minded, data conscious, inquiring. It is antimoralistic as well as antilegalistic, for it is sensitive to variety and complexity. It is neither simplistic nor perfectionist. It is "casuistry" (case-based) in a constructive and nonpejorative sense of the word. We should perhaps call it "neocasuistry." Like classical casuistry, it is case-focused and concrete, concerned to bring Christian imperatives into practical operation. But unlike classical casuistry, this neocasuistry repudiates any attempt to anticipate or prescribe real-life decisions in their existential

[19] *God in Search of Man: A Philosophy of Judaism* (Farrar, Strauss & Cudahy, Inc., 1956), p. 204.

particularity. It works with two guidelines from Paul:
"The written code kills, but the Spirit gives life" (II Cor.
3:6), and "For the whole law is fulfilled in one word,
'You shall love your neighbor as yourself' " (Gal. 5:14).

In the words of Millar Burrows' finding in Biblical
theology: "He who makes the law his standard is obligated
to perform all its precepts, for to break one commandment
is to break the law. He who lives by faith and love is not
judged on that basis, but by a standard infinitely higher
and at the same time more attainable."[20] This is why
Msgr. Pietro Palazzini (Secretary of the Sacred Congregation of the Council) freely acknowledges that situation
ethics "must not be understood as an escape from the
heavy burden of moral integrity. For, though its advocates
truly deny the absolute value of universal norms, some
are motivated by the belief that in this manner they are
better safeguarding the eminent sovereignty of God."[21]

As we shall see, *Christian* situation ethics has only one
norm or principle or law (call it what you will) that is
binding and unexceptionable, always good and right
regardless of the circumstances. That is "love"—the *agapē*
of the summary commandment to love God and the
neighbor.[22] Everything else without exception, all laws
and rules and principles and ideals and norms, are only
contingent, only valid *if they happen* to serve love in any
situation. Christian situation ethics is not a system or
program of living according to a code, but an effort to
relate love to a world of relativities through a casuistry

[20] *An Outline of Biblical Theology* (The Westminster
Press, 1946), pp. 163–164.

[21] Article, "Morality, Situation," in *Dictionary of Moral
Theology,* ed. by Francesco Cardinal Roberti and Msgr. Pietro
Palazzini (The Newman Press, 1962), pp. 800–802.

[22] Matt. 5:43–48 and ch. 22:34–40; Luke 6:27–28;
10:25–28 and vs. 29–37; Mark 12:28–34; Gal. 5:14; Rom.
13:8–10; etc.

obedient to love. It is the strategy of love. This strategy denies that there are, as Sophocles thought, any unwritten immutable laws of heaven, agreeing with Bultmann that all such notions are idolatrous and a demonic pretension.[23]

In non-Christian situation ethics some other highest good or *summum bonum* will, of course, take love's place as the one and only standard—such as self-realization in the ethics of Aristotle. But the *Christian* is neighbor-centered first and last. Love is for people, not for principles; i.e., it is personal—and therefore when the impersonal universal conflicts with the personal particular, the latter prevails in situation ethics. Because of its mediating position, prepared to act on moral laws or in spite of them, the antinomians will call situationists soft legalists, and legalists will call them cryptoantinomians.

PRINCIPLES, YES, BUT NOT RULES

It is necessary to insist that situation ethics is willing to make full and respectful use of principles, to be treated as maxims but not as laws or precepts. We might call it "principled relativism." To repeat the term used above, principles or maxims or general rules are *illuminators*. But they are not *directors*. The classic rule of moral theology has been to follow laws but do it *as much as possible* according to love and according to reason (*secundum caritatem et secundum rationem*). Situation ethics, on the other hand, calls upon us to keep law in a subservient place, so that *only* love and reason really count when the chips are down!

Situationists have no invariable obligation to what are sometimes called "middle axioms," logically derived as normative propositions based on love. An example of what is meant is the proposition that love of the neighbor in

[23] Rudolf Bultmann, *Essays Philosophical and Theological* (The Macmillan Company, 1955), pp. 22, 154.

practice *usually* means putting human rights before property rights. The term "middle axiom," first used by J. H. Oldham and William Temple, and notably by John C. Bennett in America, is well-meant but unfortunate, since an axiom is a self-validating, nonderivative proposition and it cannot stand in the "middle" between something logically prior to it and a subsequent derivative. Middle-axiom theorists must beware lest they, too, slip into the error of deriving universals from universals.

There are usually two rules of reason used in moral inquiry. One is "internal consistency," and nobody has any quarrel with it—a proposition ought not to contradict itself. The other is "external consistence" (analogy), the principle that what applies in one case should apply in all similar cases. It is around this second canon that the differences arise. Antinomians reject analogy altogether, with their doctrine of radical particularity. Situationists ask, very seriously, if there ever are enough cases enough alike to validate a law or to support anything more than a cautious generalization. In Edmond Cahn's puckish phrase, "Every case is like every other case, and no two cases are alike."[24]

There is no real quarrel here between situationism and an ethic of principles, unless the principles are hardened into laws.[25] Bishop Robinson says: "Such an ethic [situationism] cannot but rely, in deep humility, upon guiding rules, upon the cumulative experience of one's own and other people's obedience. It is this bank of experience which gives us our working rules of 'right' and 'wrong,' and without them we could not but flounder."[26] Never-

[24] "The Lawyer as Scientist and Scoundrel," *New York University Law Review*, Vol. 36 (1961), p. 10.

[25] J. M. Gustafson sees this clearly in "Context Versus Principle," *loc. cit.;* less clearly in "Christian Ethics," in *Religion*, ed. by Paul Ramsey (Prentice-Hall, Inc., 1965), pp. 285–354.

[26] *Honest to God*, pp. 119–120.

theless, in situation ethics even the most revered principles may be thrown aside if they conflict in any concrete case with love. Even Karl Barth, who writes vehemently of "absolutely wrong" actions, allows for what he calls the *ultima ratio,* the outside chance that love in a particular situation might override the absolute. The instance he gives is abortion.[27]

Using terms made popular by Tillich and others, we may say that Christian situationism is a method that proceeds, so to speak, from (1) its one and only law, *agapē* (love), to (2) the *sophia* (wisdom) of the church and culture, containing many "general rules" of more or less reliability, to (3) the *kairos* (moment of decision, the fullness of time) in which *the responsible self in the situation* decides whether the *sophia* can serve love there, or not. This is the situational strategy in capsule form. To legalists it will seem to treat the *sophia* without enough reverence and obedience; to antinomians it will appear befuddled and "inhibited" by the *sophia.*

Legalists make an idol of the *sophia,* antinomians repudiate it, situationists *use* it. They cannot give to any principle less than love more than tentative consideration, for they know, with Dietrich Bonhoeffer, "The question of the good is posed and is decided in the midst of each definite, yet unconcluded, unique and transient situation of our lives, in the midst of our living relationships with men, things, institutions and powers, in other words in the midst of our historical existence."[28] And Bonhoeffer, of course, is a modern Christian ethicist who was himself executed for trying to kill, even *murder,* Adolf Hitler— so far did he go as a situationist.

In Europe representative situationists in theological ethics are Brunner, Barth, Bonhoeffer, Niels Søe, Bult-

---

[27] *Church Dogmatics* (Edinburgh: T. & T. Clark, 1961), Vol. III, Bk. 4, pp. 420–421.
[28] *Ethics,* p. 185.

mann. In America we may mention H. R. Niebuhr,
Joseph Sittler, James Gustafson, Paul Lehmann, Gordon
Kaufman, Charles West, and this writer. We may certainly add Tillich. They have been criticized for a too
radical rejection of moral laws and principles, especially
by John Bennett, James Adams, Paul Ramsey, Robert
Fitch, Clinton Gardiner, and Edward Long, in America,
and by more conservative writers in Europe such as
Werner Elert.[29] Among Roman Catholic scholars, committed to opposing situation ethics by Pope Pius XII, we
might cite Karl Rahner, S.J., in Europe and Robert
Gleason, S.J., in America. The theological or philosophical
framework is not the same for any of these people, but
it need not be, since situationism is a *method,* not a substantive ethic.

There has indeed been a "misplaced debate" about
situation ethics, because so many have too quickly taken
it to be *antinomian.* Their error, due to the oversimple
judgment of some European theologians, appeared offi-
cially first in an allocution of Pius XII on April 18, 1952,
in which the terms "existential" and "situational" were
made synonymous.[30] It was pointed out that as a warning
such an ethic could be used to justify birth control. Four
years later *"Situations-ethik"* was labeled "the new morality" (February 2, 1956, the Supreme Sacred Congregation of the Holy Office) and banned from all academies
and seminaries. This confusion of situation ethics and
existential ethics appeared in Protestant circles as well.[31]
An occasional Anglican writer does the same thing.[32] Paul

[29] Cf. bibliography in Gustafson, "Context Versus Principle," *loc. cit.,* pp. 171–173.

[30] *Acta Apostolicae Sedis,* Vol. 44 (1952), pp. 413–519.

[31] W. Burnett Easton, Jr., "Ethical Relativism and Popular
Morality," *Theology Today,* Vol. 14 (1958), pp. 470–477.

[32] J. H. Jacques, *The Right and the Wrong* (London:
S.P.C.K., 1964), p. 13.

Ramsey is a distinguished perpetrator of this misplaced argument in America.[33]

No doubt some early situationists were not easily distinguishable from existential or antinomian writers. This was true of certain German Catholics (e.g., E. Michel and Theodore Steinbüchel), and certainly of the German Protestant Eberhard Griesbach (*Gegenwart, eine kritische Ethik;* Halle, 1928). Many Christian ethicists in recent years, both Catholic and Protestant, have tried to deal somewhat more carefully with the issues at stake. The theologian Jacques Leclercq has reasoned that the classic virtue of prudence, like Aristotle's *epieikeia* (equity), justifies situationism.[34] Matthew Arnold rendered *epieikeia* as "sweet reasonableness." Another Catholic, the lay scholar Josef Pieper, has developed the point: "The statements of moral theology, including those of casuistry, necessarily remain general. They can never take hold of a real and whole 'here and now' for the reason that only the person engaged in decision experiences (or at least *can* experience) the concrete situation with its need for concrete action. He alone."[35] He adds, "Prudence is the mould of the virtues; but charity is the mould even of prudence itself." Here we have echoes of the prudence-based casuistry of some earlier moralists called "compensationism."[36]

In the spirit of *aggiornamento,* the Jesuit theologian Karl Rahner, for example, is trying to ease the strictures

[33] "Faith Effective Through In-Principled Love," *Christianity and Crisis,* Vol. XX (1960), pp. 76–78.

[34] *Christ and the Modern Conscience,* tr. by Ronald Matthews (London: Geoffrey Chapman, Ltd., 1962), p. 126.

[35] *Prudence* (London: Faber & Faber, Ltd., 1959), pp. 45, 48.

[36] Cf. T. P. Coffee, "Moral Systems and a Defense of Compensationism," *Anglican Theological Review,* Vol. XLI (1959), pp. 199–211.

of the "natural law" and of canon law. "In principle," he believes, "there can in one and the same situation be several possibilities of action, not only practical but justified. The choice between these possibilities, which has to be made and always involves an historical human decision, cannot, in principle, be settled in advance in the name of Christianity."[37] There is no reduction of law to a subservient role, here, nor any abandonment of the notion that things are intrinsically right or wrong, but Rahner's discussion *is* a serious and sincere probing of the issue raised by situation ethics.

The basic legalism of classical Christian ethics will resist the situational love ethic by any and every tactic. Nevertheless, the growing jeopardy of law-ethics is clear. We need only to recall how the dean of Anglican moral theologians, Bishop Kenneth Kirk, ended his effort to be a casuist, a *practical* moralist. Pointing out that at most the number of unalterable principles must be "very small," Kirk admitted that "if we followed out this line of thought to the end (as has rarely been done in Christian ethics), there could strictly speaking be only one such principle. For if any principle has an inalienable right to be observed, *every* other principle would have to be waived if the two came into conflict in a given case."[38] *Exactly!* Christian ethics has indeed failed to follow up that line of thought! But situation ethics picks it up. It holds flatly that there is only one principle, love, without any prefabricated recipes for what it means in practice, and that *all other* so-called principles or maxims are relative to particular, concrete situations! If it has any rules, they are only rules of thumb.

Kirk mourned, further, that "it seems that we have reached a point at which the whole ambitious structure

[37] *The Christian Commitment* (London: Sheed & Ward, Ltd., 1963), pp. 7–8.

[38] *Conscience and Its Problems* (London: Longmans, Green & Co., Ltd., 1927), p. 331.

of moral theology is revealed as a complete futility. Every man must decide for himself according to his own estimate of conditions and consequences; and no one can decide for him or impugn the decision to which he comes. Perhaps this is the end of the matter after all."[39] *This is precisely what this book is intended to show.*

ABORTION: A SITUATION

In 1962 a patient in a state mental hospital raped a fellow patient, an unmarried girl ill with a radical schizophrenic psychosis. The victim's father, learning what had happened, charged the hospital with culpable negligence and requested that an abortion to end the unwanted pregnancy be performed at once, in an early stage of the embryo. The staff and administrators of the hospital refused to do so, on the ground that the criminal law forbids all abortion except "therapeutic" ones when the mother's life is at stake—because the *moral* law, it is supposed, holds that any interference with an embryo after fertilization is murder, i.e., the taking of an innocent human being's life.

Let's relate the three ethical approaches to this situation. The rape has occurred and the decisional question is: May we rightly (licitly) terminate this pregnancy, begun in an act of force and violence by a mentally unbalanced rapist upon a frightened, mentally sick girl? Mother and embryo are apparently healthy on all the usual counts.

The legalists would say *NO*. Their position is that killing is absolutely wrong, inherently evil. It is permissible only as self-defense and in military service, which is held to be presumptive self-defense or justifiable homicide. If the mother's life is threatened, abortion is therefore justified, but for no other reasons. (Many doctors take an elastic view of "life" and thereby justify abortions to save

[39] *Ibid.*, pp. 375–376.

a patient's *mental* life as well as physical.) Even in cases where they justify it, it is only *excused*—it is still held to be inherently evil. Many Protestants hold this view, and some humanists.

Catholic moral theology goes far beyond even the rigid legalism of the criminal law, absolutizing their prohibition of abortion *absolutely*, by denying all exceptions and calling even therapeutic abortion wrong. (They allow killing in self-defense against malicious, i.e., deliberate, aggressors but not in self-defense against innocent, i.e., unintentional aggressors.) Thus if it is a tragic choice of the mother's life or the baby's, as can happen in rare cases, neither can be saved.

To this ethical nightmare legalism replies: "It is here that the Church appears merciless, but she is not. It is her logic which is merciless; and she promises that if the logic is followed the woman will receive a reward far greater than a number of years of life."[40] Inexplicably, shockingly, Dietrich Bonhoeffer says the same thing: "The life of the mother is in the hand of God, but the life of the child is arbitrarily extinguished. The question whether the life of the mother or the life of the child is of greater value can hardly be a matter for a human decision."[41]

The antinomians—but who can predict what *they* would say? Their ethic is by its nature and definition outside the reach of even generalities. We can only guess, not unreasonably, that if the antinomian lives by a love norm, he will be apt to favor abortion in this case.

The situationists, if their norm is the Christian commandment to love the neighbor, would almost certainly, *in this case*, favor abortion and support the girl's father's request. (Many purely humanistic decision makers are of

[40] Alan Keenan, O.F.M., and John Ryan, M.D., *Marriage: A Medical and Sacramental Study* (Sheed & Ward, Inc., 1955), p. 53.

[41] *Ethics*, p. 131n.

the same mind about abortion following rape, and after incest too.) They would in all likelihood favor abortion for the sake of the patient's physical and mental health, not only if it were needed to save her life. It is even likely they would favor abortion for the sake of the victim's self-respect or reputation or happiness or simply on the ground that *no unwanted and unintended* baby should ever be born.

They would, one hopes, reason that it is *not* killing because there is no person or human life in an embryo at an early stage of pregnancy (Aristotle and St. Thomas held that opinion), or even if it *were* killing, it would not be murder because it is self-defense against, in this case, not one but *two* aggressors. First there is the rapist, who being insane was morally and legally innocent, and then there is the "innocent" embryo which is continuing the ravisher's original aggression! Even self-defense legalism would have allowed the girl to kill her attacker, no matter that he was innocent in the forum of conscience because of his madness. The embryo is no more innocent, no less an aggressor or unwelcome invader! Is not the most loving thing possible (the right thing) in this case a responsible decision to terminate the pregnancy?

What think ye?

II

Some Presuppositions

THE HEART OF THIS explanation of situation ethics lies in its six propositions. They will be set forth to show how love works in ethical decision-making. But there are a few preliminary matters to be made plain first, in the reader's interest, so that he can know what *presuppositions* are at work. There are four of them. If need be, then, he can correct for any bias he thinks they are imposing. Their labels look far more technical and up in the air than they really are.

FOUR WORKING PRINCIPLES

1. *Pragmatism*

In the first place, this book is consciously inspired by American *pragmatism*. Forty years ago when the author became a theological student, he was a professed advocate of the Peirce-James-Dewey analysis of human knowledge. But soon the long threads of tradition and the honeyed discourse of those who purvey the perennial philosophy sold him on the notion that metaphysics was, after all, a vehicle able to carry us across the gulf from skepticism to faith. This reversion to classical philosophy was successfully engineered, even though he knew that philosophizing had never managed to carry William James to faith (he remained nontheologically "religious" to the end), while

Charles Sanders Peirce and John Dewey, each in his own way, stayed steadfastly both nontheological *and* nonreligious.[1]

Coming full circle once again, this writer now recognizes, but more maturely, that philosophy is utterly useless as a way to bridge the gap between doubt and faith. And along with this neopragmatism, congenially, he has appreciated in a more sophisticated way the importance of the contextual or situational, i.e., the *circumstantial* approach to the search for the right and the good. We have seen the light when we recognize that abstract and conceptual morality is a mare's nest. Bonhoeffer was correct in his distaste for metaphysics, as Kierkegaard was in his hatred of systems.

Let us pinpoint this pragmatism before we move on. For our purposes here, let's just say that the pragmatic method is a legitimate tool of ethics. American pragmatism and British empiricism have always trained their sights primarily on Pilate's question, "What is truth?" The ethical question, on the other hand, is, What is good? Yet the *verum* and the *bonum* (and for that matter, the *pulchrum* as well) are not really separable matters. James said, "The true, to put it briefly, is only the expedient in our way of thinking, just as the right is only the expedient in the way of our behaving."[2] (This is the same temper and the very term Paul uses in I Cor. 6:12, when he says anything could be "lawful" but only if it is "expedient," i.e., constructive or upbuilding.)

As James called truth and goodness expediency, so John Dewey saw them as what gives *satisfaction,* and

[1] See Peirce's *Chance Love and Logic,* ed. by Morris Cohen (Harcourt, Brace & Co., 1923), and Dewey's *A Common Faith* (Yale University Press, 1934).

[2] *Pragmatism* (Longmans, Green & Co., Inc., 1907), p. 222; repeated *The Meaning of Truth* (Longmans, Green & Co., Inc., 1929), p. vii.

F. C. S. Schiller as what *works*.[3] All are agreed: the good
is what works, what is expedient, what gives satisfaction.
Socrates' question, "What is goodness?" gets from pragmatism the same answer Pilate's does. The good, it replies,
like the true, is whatever works.

As Bonhoeffer said, "To ignore the ethical significance
of success is to betray . . . a defective sense of responsibility."[4] Pragmatism is, to be plainspoken, a *practical* or
success posture. Its idiom expresses the genius and ethos
or style of life of American culture and of the techno-
scientific era. Whereas classical ethics and aesthetics
treated the good and the beautiful separately (in spite of
the Greeks' *kalos* which coalesces them), pragmatism lumps
them *and* the cognitive all together, all three, under one
broad umbrella—value. This puts the ethical question in
the chair, at the head of the conference table.

We must realize, however, that pragmatism, as such, is
no self-contained world view. It is a method, precisely. It
is not a substantive faith, and properly represented it
never pretends to be. Pragmatism of itself yields none of
the norms we need to measure or verify the very success
that pragmatism calls for! To be correct or right a thing—
a thought or an action—must *work*. Yes. But work to what
end, for what purpose, to satisfy what standard or ideal
or norm? Like any other method, pragmatism as such is
utterly without any way of answering this question. Yet
this is the decisive question.

The very first question in all ethics is, *What* do I want?
Only after this is settled (pleasure in hedonism, adjust-

[3] See Dewey's *The Quest for Certainty* (Minton, Balch &
Co., 1929) and *Ethics,* with J. H. Tufts (Henry Holt,
1908); F.C.S. Schiller's *Problems of Belief* (London: Hodder & Stoughton, Ltd., 1924); G. H. Mead's *Mind, Self, and
Society* (1934) and *The Philosophy of the Act* (1938), both
ed. by C. W. Morris (The University of Chicago Press).

[4] *Letters and Papers from Prison,* tr. by Reginald Fuller
(The Macmillan Company, 1962), p. 21.

ment in naturalism, self-realization in eudaemonism, etc.) can we ask about the *why* and the *how* and the *who* and the *when* and the *where* and the *which!* The primary issue is the "value" problem, our choice of our *summum bonum*. This is a *pre*ethical or metaethical question, relying on some other source for a faith proposition or commitment. Only after this is settled can the method go to work, only after it knows *what* it is to seek or serve.

Christianly speaking, as we shall see, the norm or measure by which any thought or action is to be judged a success or failure, i.e., right or wrong, is *love*. What "love" is can wait for later and longer discussion, but here and now let it be clear that the situationist, whether a Christian or not, follows a strategy that is pragmatic.

In James's words: "A pragmatist turns his back resolutely and once for all upon a lot of inveterate habits dear to professional philosophers. He turns away from abstraction and insufficiency, from verbal solutions, from bad a priori reasons, from fixed principles, closed systems, and pretended absolutes and origins. He turns toward concreteness and adequacy, toward facts, toward actions, and toward power."[5]

2. *Relativism*

In our attempt to be situational, to be contemporary in our understanding of conscience, we can pin another label on our method. It is *relativistic*. As the strategy is pragmatic, the tactics are relativistic. Perhaps the most pervasive culture trait of the scientific era and of contemporary man is the relativism with which everything is seen and understood. Our thought forms are relativistic to a degree that our forefathers never imagined. We have become fully and irreversibly "contingent," not only about our particular ideas, but about the very idea of ideas themselves (cognitive value) and about goodness itself (moral value). The situationist avoids words like "never" and

[5] *Pragmatism*, p. 51.

"perfect" and "always" and "complete" as he avoids the plague, as he avoids "absolutely."

In a symposium on anthropology Lynn White describes four major shifts in the canons of culture.[6] All of them move in the direction of relativity. They are: (1) the shift from an Occidental to a global outlook, in which cultures are no longer compared as "high" and "low" (Europe's usually at the top!) but by purely factual and descriptive differences, unprejudiced; (2) the shift from language and logic to the use of symbol and nondiscursive reasoning;[7] (3) the shift away from the rules of rationality to acceptance of unconscious and motivational dynamics as the foundation of human behavior; and (4) the shift—which is clearly visible in any situation ethic—from a hierarchy of values, ranged in some supposedly "given" and permanent order of bad or better, to a fluid *spectrum* of values.

This last shift is often mere drift, uncritically forsaking the idea that some things are better than others and adopting the notion that they are merely different, shading back and forth into each other according to the situation or the culture context—or even according to one's personal taste subjectively. With some this takes the radical form of *De gustibus non disputandum,* so that "What's one man's meat is another man's poison" in a kind of "absolute relativism."

To be relative, of course, means to be relative *to* something. To be "absolutely relative" (an uneasy combination of terms) is to be inchoate, random, unpredictable, unjudgeable, meaningless, amoral—rather in the antinomian mode. There must be an absolute or norm of some kind if there is to be any true relativity. This is the

---

[6] *Frontiers of Knowledge in the Study of Man* (Harper & Brothers, 1956), pp. 302–315.

[7] E.g., "symbol" in the myth concept of Biblical theologians and political scientists; "nondiscursive reason" in Zen literature, nonobjective art, and Gestalt psychology.

central fact in the normative relativism of a situation ethic. It is not anarchic (i.e., without an *archē*, an ordering principle). In *Christian* situationism the ultimate criterion is, as we shall be seeing, "agapeic love." It relativizes the absolute, it does not absolutize the relative!

The word "context" is almost a fetish nowadays, and a culturally revealing verbal trait. ("We have to see it in its context," people say of everything. Their stress is on *Sitz-im-leben*—as in Biblical hermeneutics.) It shows our sharp sense of relativity and a far greater *humility* than ever emerged in the classical intellectual tradition. The same temper makes us more dialectical than men of the past, recognizing polarities rather than either-ors. In Christian ethics the three polarities of law and love, of authority and experience, and of fixity and freedom are "fruitful tensions" typical of contemporary discussion. The first one, law and love, is the predominant issue posed by the Christian form of situation ethics but all three are at stake in *all* forms of situation method.

Ethical relativism has invaded Christian ethics progressively ever since the simultaneous appearance in 1932 of Emil Brunner's *The Divine Imperative* and Reinhold Niebuhr's *Moral Man and Immoral Society*.[8] Both theologians built their conceptions of the Christian ethic on the principle that the divine command is always the same in its *Why* but always different in its *What,* or changeless as to the *What* but contingent as to the *How.* We are always, that is to say, commanded to act lovingly, but how to do it depends on our own *responsible* estimate of the situation. Only love is a constant; everything else is a variable. The shift to relativism carries contemporary Christians away from code ethics, away from stern ironbound do's and don'ts, away from prescribed conduct and legalistic morality.

The Pharisees' kind of ethics, Torah, is now suffering a second eclipse, a far more radical one than it endured

[8] Charles Scribner's Sons, 1932.

under Jesus' and Paul's attacks. Our milieu and era are far
unfriendlier to law ethics than were the apostolic and
patristic times, to say nothing of the medieval period. "The
truth of ethical relativism," says Paul Tillich, "lies in the
moral laws' inability to give commandments which are
unambiguous both in their general form and in their
concrete applications. Every moral law is abstract in relation to the unique and totally concrete situation. This is
true of what has been called natural law and of what has
been called revealed law."[9]

Contemporary Christians should not underestimate this
relativism, in either its secular or its Christian form. Christian ethics was drawn into it long ago when Jesus attacked
the Pharisees' principle of statutory morality, and by Paul's
rebellious appeal to grace and freedom. Even earlier, the
Biblical doctrine of man as only a finite creature of
imperfect powers and perceptions was voiced in the *docta
ignorantia* of Isa. 55:8: "For my thoughts are not your
thoughts, neither are your ways my ways, says the Lord."
This concept of human creatureliness at the very heart of
Christian ethics cries, "Relativity!" in the face of all smug
pretensions to truth and righteousness. Christians cannot
go on trying to "lay down the law" theologically, about
either creed or code.

3. *Positivism*

A third presupposition is "positivism." In the case of
Christian ethics this means theological positivism. When
we get right down to it there are really only two ways to
approach "religious knowledge" or belief—two kinds of
theological epistemology.[10] One is theological *naturalism,*
in which reason adduces or deduces faith propositions

[9] *Systematic Theology* (The Chicago University Press,
1963), Vol. III, p. 47.

[10] John B. Cobb, Jr., suggests a third, "existentialist," in his
Living Options in Protestant Theology: A Survey of Methods
(The Westminster Press, 1962) but it lacks discrete shape.

from human experience and natural phenomena; nature yields the evidences, natural reason grasps them. Natural theology, so-called, and "natural law" ethics are examples of this method.

The other approach is theological *positivism* (or "positive theology"), in which faith propositions are "posited" or affirmed voluntaristically rather than rationalistically. It is a-rational but not ir-rational, outside reason but not against it. Its starting point is like Anselm's *Credo ut intelligam* in the *Proslogion* (first chapter); thinking supported by faith rather than faith supported by thinking. Although it does not exclude reason, reason goes to work because of the commitment and in its service. Thus Christian ethics "posits" faith in God and *reasons* out what obedience to his commandment to love requires in any situation. God's existence and belief that Christ is God in man cannot be proved, any more than a Marxist can prove that history is headed for Communism and that labor is the sole source of commodity value.

But how, then, does positive thought play a part in *non*-Christian ethics? There is nothing "fideistic" or "heuristic" about the simple hedonism of a Hugh Hefner (editor of *Playboy*) or the complex social hedonism (utilitarianism) of a John Stuart Mill, or so it would seem. *But hold on!* Any moral or value judgment in ethics, like a theologian's faith proposition, is a *decision*—not a conclusion. It is a choice, not a result reached by force of logic, Q.E.D. The hedonist cannot "prove" that pleasure is the highest good, any more than the Christian can "prove" his faith that *love* is! After all, in his treatise on love, Bernard of Clairvaux found he had to declare, "*Amo quia amo*" (I love because I love). Love like good itself is axiomatic, ostensive, categorical, like blue or sour or anything else that simply is what it is, a "primary" not definable in terms of something else. There is no way under heaven of proving that the Supreme Court was "right" in decreeing in 1954 that public schools "should" and "must" ignore racial differences in their admissions policies. This is why the end product of the judicial procedure is called a *decision,* not a conclusion. Reason can note facts and infer relations, but it cannot find values (goodness). Bertrand Russell, acknowledging the nonrational nature of norms, even declares, "I can say that what the world needs is Christian love, or compassion."[11]

As a matter of fact, this limitation on logic holds in aesthetics, the search for the beautiful, as it does in ethics, the search for the good. The *pulchrum* and the *bonum* are alike; art values and moral values lie in the same field as far as logic's ground rules are concerned. Aesthetic and ethical propositions are like faith propositions, they are based upon *choice* and *decision.* The "leap of affirmation" is essential to all three.[12] (German existentialists call it *Sprung*—in which free act becomes concrete.)

Value choices are made and normative standards embraced in a fashion every bit as arbitrary and absurd as the leap of faith. The point is that nobody since Kant's analysis has seriously tried to continue Hegel's rational or "natural" demonstrations of theism except in the official Catholic Thomist line. (But even there it is only laid down as "an article of faith" that proofs of God *can* be demonstrated, not that any one of the classic "proofs" has succeeded!) Just as we cannot by reason build a bridge from the shore of doubt to the shore of faith, or from hope to certainty, or from nature to grace, so we cannot build by logic a bridge from facts to values, from isness to oughtness. Anselm's *Credo ut intelligam* has as its partner *Credo ut judiceam* (I believe so that I can make value judgments).

Ethical decisions seek justification, whereas cognitive

[11] *Human Society in Ethics and Politics* (The New American Library of World Literature, Inc., 1962), p. viii.

[12] Cf. Herbert Feigel, "De Principiis Non Disputandum," in *Philosophical Analysis,* ed. by Max Black (Prentice-Hall, Inc., 1963), pp. 113–147.

conclusions seek verification. We cannot verify moral choices. They may be vindicated, but not validated. It was David Hume who set out this elementary point in its enduring form for British and American thinking.[13] Believers or unbelievers (theologically speaking), we are all bound to acknowledge that we simply cannot climb across the gap from descriptive to prescriptive propositions; from "is" statements to "ought" statements. We have to make jumps, faith leaps. They are not steps in logic or even in common sense.

In moral theology, or, if you prefer, theological morals or Christian ethics, the key category of love (*agapē*) as the axiomatic value is established by *deciding* to say, "Yea" to the faith assertion that "God is love" and thence by logic's inference to the value assertion that love is the highest good. "You can't prove the supreme norm of an ethical system (*sic*) by deducing it from any higher norm," says John Hospers, "for if you could, it couldn't be called the supreme norm."[14] This applies to *any* ethic of whatever kind.

The faith comes first. The Johannine proposition (I John 4: 7–12) is not that God is *love* but that *God* is love! The Christian does not understand God in terms of love; he understands love in terms of God as seen in Christ. "We love, because he first loved us." This obviously is a faith foundation for love. Paul's phrase (Gal. 5:6), "faith working through love," is the essence and pith of Christian ethics. *Nevertheless,* a perfectly sincere man, in every way as intelligent and wise as any Christian might be, can refuse to put any stock whatever in Christ, in which case he might in all seriousness also doubt the hope and love that Paul linked to faith in his triad of theological

[13] *A Treatise of Human Nature* (1739), ed. by T. H. Green and T. H. Grose (London: Longmans, Green & Co., 1874), Vol. II, pp. 245–246.

[14] *Human Conduct* (Harcourt, Brace and World, Inc., 1961), p. 584.

virtues (I Cor., ch. 13). But still, these are the faith commitments which identify the Christian.

4. *Personalism*

Ethics deals with human relations.[15] Situation ethics puts people at the center of concern, not things. Obligation is to persons, not to things; to subjects, not objects. The legalist is a *what* asker (What does the law say?); the situationist is a *who* asker (Who is to be helped?). That is, situationists are *personalistic*. In the Christian version, for example, a basic maxim is that the disciple is commanded to love people, not principles or laws or objects or any other *thing*.

There are no "values" in the sense of inherent goods— value is what *happens to* something when it happens to be useful to love working for the sake of persons. Brunner declared that the notion of value apart from persons is a "phantasmagoria."[16] There are no intrinsic values, he says, being a blunt situationist. Anything, material or immaterial, is "good" only because it is good for or to somebody. (Pius XII warned against "personalistic morality," but its influence continues to grow among Catholic theologians.[17])

And just as good derives from the needs of people, so people derive from society. There is nothing individualistic about personalism, nor in situation ethics. *Ein Mensch ist kein Mensch* (A solitary man is no man at all). *Value is relative to persons and persons are relative to society, to neighbors.* An I is an I in relationship with a *You*; a *You* is a *You*, capable of being an I, in relation to a *Me*. Martin Buber's "dialogic" thesis about *I-Thou*—i.e., that true existence lies in personal relationships, not in *I-it*

[15] A fine essay on ethics as relational is H. R. Niebuhr, "The Center of Value," *Moral Principles of Action,* ed. by R. N. Anshen (Harper & Brothers, 1952), pp. 162–175.

[16] *The Divine Imperative,* p. 194.

[17] *Acta Apostolicae Sedis,* Vol. 45 (1953), p. 278.

(relation to mere things)—has greatly influenced man theory in such theological work as Maritain's, Berdyaev's, and Tillich's.[18] Only people can exercise the freedom that is essential in the forum of conscience for decision-making. Only free persons, capable of being "the responsible self," can sustain relationship and thereby enter the field of obligation.

In *Christian* situation ethics, there is also a theological side to personalism, since God is "personal" and has created men in his own image—*imago Dei.* Personality is *therefore* the first-order concern in ethical choices. Kant's second maxim holds: Treat persons as ends, never as means. Even if in some situations a material thing is chosen rather than a person, it will be (if it is Christianly done) for the sake of the person, not for the sake of the thing itself. If a man prefers to keep his money invested instead of giving it to his son who needs it, it could only be because he believes his son will need it far more urgently later on. To repeat, values are only extrinsically, never intrinsically, "valuable." Love is of people, by people, and for people. Things are to be used; people are to be loved. It is "immoral" when people are used and things are loved. Loving actions are the *only* conduct permissible.

The Christian situationist says to the non-Christian situationist who is also neighbor—or person—concerned: "*Your* love is like mine, like everybody's; it is the Holy Spirit. Love is not the work of the Holy Spirit, it *is* the Holy Spirit—working in us. God *is* love, he doesn't merely *have* it or *give* it; he gives himself—to all men, to all sorts and conditions: to believers and unbelievers, high and low, dark and pale, learned and ignorant, Marxists and Christians and Hottentots."

[18] Cf. Will Herberg, *Four Existentialist Theologians* (Doubleday & Company, Inc., 1958), and J. B. Coates, *The Crisis of the Human Person* (Longmans, Green & Co., Inc., 1949).

This is what is meant by "uncovenanted" grace. This is the "saving" truth about themselves which the faithless, alas, do not grasp! It is not the unbelieving who invite "damnation" but the unloving. Temple insisted that "the atheist who is moved by love is moved by the spirit of God; an atheist who lives by love is saved by his faith in the God whose existence (under that name) he denies."[19]

If we put these working principles together (pragmatism, relativism, positivism, and personalism), their shape is obviously one of action, *existence*, eventfulness. The situation ethic, unlike some other kinds, is an ethic of *decision*—of *making* decisions rather than "looking them up" in a manual of prefab rules. Goethe's "In the beginning was the deed" comes to mind. James A. Pike's book title, *Doing the Truth*, puts it in a nutshell.[20] Situation ethics is more Biblical and verb-thinking than Greek and noun-thinking. It does not ask *what* is good but *how* to do good for *whom;* not what *is* love but how to *do* the most loving thing possible in the situation. It focuses upon *pragma* (doing), not upon *dogma* (some tenet). Its concern is with behaving according to the believing. It is an activity, not a feeling, an "activistic" ethic. Kant's phrase for ethics, "practical reason," is precisely correct. We can agree with G. E. Moore at least about this: that "casuistry is the goal of ethical investigation"—i.e., that an ethic is inauthentic until it gets down to cases.[21]

CONSCIENCE

Situation ethics is interested in conscience (moral consciousness) as a function, not as a faculty. It takes conscience into account only when it is working, practicing,

[19] *Nature, Man and God,* p. 416.

[20] *Doing the Truth,* rev. ed. (The Macmillan Company, 1965).

[21] *Principia Ethica* (Cambridge: Cambridge University Press, 1960), p. 5.

deciding. There have been four theories about what "conscience" is, but situationism takes none of them seriously. Some have said it is an innate, radarlike, built-in faculty —intuition. Others have thought of it as inspiration from outside the decision maker—guidance by the Holy Spirit or a guardian angel or a Jiminy Cricket. The popular theory nowadays is "introjection"—that conscience is the internalized value system of the culture and society. The Thomists have followed Aquinas' definition, that it is the reason making moral judgments or value choices.[22] But situationism has no ontology or being theory for conscience, whatsoever.[23]

The traditional error lies in thinking about conscience as a noun instead of as a verb. This reflects the fixity and establishment-mindedness of all law ethics as contrasted to love ethics. There *is* no conscience; "conscience" is merely a word for our attempts to make decisions creatively, constructively, fittingly. If, with Huckleberry Finn, we were to suppose that conscience is a faculty, with a bag of reliable rules and principles, then we should have to say what Huck said when he wrestled over whether it was right to befriend Jim, the runaway slave: "If I had a yaller dog that didn't know more than a person's conscience does, I would pison him. It takes up more room than all the rest of a person's insides, and yet ain't no good, nohow. Tom Sawyer he says the same."[24] Thomas Aquinas' description is the best (leaving aside his faculty idea): the reason making moral judgments.

[22] Thomas tied conscience to a faculty, synteresis; for a critique, see Eric D'Arcy, *Conscience and the Right to Freedom* (London: Sheed & Ward, Ltd., 1961).

[23] Martin Heidegger calls conscience "the call of Nothing," i.e., of the ultimate in the finite. It is *nothing,* all right: no thing! Cf. *Being and Time* (Harper & Row, Publishers, Inc., 1962), pp. 312–348.

[24] *The Complete Works of Mark Twain,* ed. by Charles Neider (Doubleday & Company, Inc., 1964), Vol. I, p. 921.

Another feature of situation ethics is its concern with antecedent rather than consequent conscience, i.e., with prospective decision-making rather than with retrospective judgment-passing. The ancient world ordinarily thought of conscience (*syneidēsis*) as a review officer, weighing an action ex post facto and rendering approval or disapproval. (We all do this, head on pillow, after a long, hard day!) An example is Ernest Hemingway's famous definition, "What's good is what I feel good after, and what's bad is what I feel bad after." Savage cultures have often thought of conscience with the model of a sharp stone in the breast under the sternum, which turns and hurts when we have done wrong. Conscience here is remorse or reassurance.

Paul spoke of conscience in two of his letters, to Rome and Corinth, and tended to give a new twist to the Greco-Roman idea by treating it as a *director* of human decisions rather than simply a reviewer.[25] It acquired a future reference, directive and not merely reactive. So it is with situation ethics. By contrast, the morality of the confessional is ex post facto and retrospective, backward-looking.

Historically, man's ethical struggle (including Christian ethics) has worked out theories in the abstract about the nature of the good and about right conduct. It has tried, then, to apply these theories as rules prescribing actions. Christian thought and practice, for example, has tackled Christian ethics first, elaborating the *ideal* as based on systems of Biblical, historical, and dogmatic theology. The second stage has been moral theology, an attempt to formulate and articulate (i.e., systematize) working principles or rules, from the ideal. The third stage has been to use these rules and principles as prescriptions and directives in actual cases (casuistry).

This strategy produced a bed of Procrustes onto which the decisions of life had to be forced and cut to fit the bed's

[25] C. A. Pierce, *Conscience in the New Testament* (London: Alec R. Allenson, Inc., 1955), pp. 84–90.

iron shape and size. The *aggiornamento* spirit has led
Father C. E. Curran to speak of a "need for a life-centered
and not a confession-oriented moral theology," explaining
that "theologians have begun to react against the manualis-
tic treatment of conscience." "God," he says, "has called
each person by his own name. In one sense, every individual is unique; every concrete situation is unique. . . .
Frequently there are no easy solutions. After prayerful
consideration of all values involved, the Christian chooses
what he believes to be the demands of love in the present
situation."[26]

The pragmatic-empirical temper of situation ethics, on
the other hand, calls for a radical reversal of the classic
approach. It focuses on cases and tries experientially, not
propositionally, to adduce, not deduce, some "general"
ideas to be held only tentatively and lightly. It deals with
cases in all their contextual particularity, deferring in fear
and trembling only to the rule of love. Situation ethics
keeps principles sternly in their place, in the role of advisers without veto power!

Only one "general" proposition is prescribed, namely,
the commandment to love God through the neighbor.
"God does not will to draw any love exclusively to Himself;
He wills that we should love Him 'in our neighbor.' "[27]
And this commandment is, be it noted, a normative ideal;
it is *not* an operational directive. All else, all other generalities (e.g., "One should tell the truth" and "One should
respect life") are at most only *maxims,* never rules. For
the situationist there are no rules—none at all.

[26] "The Problem of Conscience and the Twentieth Century
Christian," in *Ecumenical Dialogue,* ed. by S. H. Miller and
G. E. Wright (Harvard University Press, 1964), pp. 262–
273.
[27] Brunner, *The Divine Imperative,* p. 133. "The love of
God, His surrender of Himself to man, comes to meet us in
the Man Jesus. To love man means to be united to him in
love. This alone is the Good."

Now let us turn to the main body of this book, to the six propositions upon which it rests. The first one pins down the nature of value. The second reduces all values to love. The third equates love and justice. The fourth frees love from sentimentality. The fifth states the relation between means and ends. The sixth authenticates every decision within its own context.

From this point on we will be speaking of *Christian* situation ethics, even though many of the things said about it apply fully as much to others whose method of decision-making is, like ours, both nonlegalistic and person-centered rather than principle-centered.

III

Love Only Is Always Good

The First Proposition: "Only one 'thing' is intrinsically good; namely, love: nothing else at all."

THE ROCK-BOTTOM issue in all ethics is "value." Where is it, what is its locus? Is the worthiness or worthness of a thing inherent *in* it? Or is it contingent, *relative* to other things than itself? Is the good or evil of a thing, and the right or wrong of an action, intrinsic or extrinsic?

NOMINAL GOOD

The medieval realist-nominalist debate, in part carried on around this basic question of ethical understanding, is by no means merely archaic or an outworn argument. Everything hangs on it, as we saw in the preceding chapter. For an intelligent adult grasp of the problems of ethics it is *this* question which has to be settled first. It is a most pervasive issue in Christian ethics even if it lurks mostly beneath the surface, unrecognized by the simpleminded. Ockham and Scotus in the Middle Ages, and Descartes in modern times, postulated the view that any "good" is nominal, i.e., it is what it is only because God regards it as good. This was opposed to the "realist" view that God wills a thing because it *is* good. God finds "valuable" whatever suits his (love's) needs and purposes. Situation ethics,

at the level of human value judgments, is likewise nomin-
alistic. (A non-Christian version may be seen in Charles
Stevenson's *Ethics and Language*.[1])

The whole mind-set of the modern man, *our* mind-set,
is on the nominalists' side. No better example can be
found than Brunner's flat assertion that there are no intrinsic values and that value exists only "in reference to
persons."[2] Martin Buber is equally plain about it; he says
that "value is always value for a person rather than something with an absolute, independent existence."[3] Another
kind of personalist, a very metaphysical one, Edgar Bright-
man, argued that "in personality is the only true intrinsic
value we know or could conceive; all values are but forms
of personal experience."[4] There *are* no "values" at all;
there are only things (material and nonmaterial) which
happen to be valued by persons. This is the personalist
view.

Temple's way of putting it was that value, like revelation, "depends for its actuality upon the appreciating
mind."[5] In another place he concludes: "Value, as it appears to me, consists in an interaction of mind and environment, but always of such a kind that the mind is
finding in the environment the objective occasion for its
own satisfaction."[6] In his attempt to define the good
Christologically, Dietrich Bonhoeffer came close to seeing
the "property versus predicate" issue, but he fell short, he
missed it.[7] On this score, as on so many others, we see how

[1] *Yale University Press,* 1944, esp. ch. viii.

[2] *The Divine Imperative,* pp. 194–195.

[3] See Maurice B. Friedman, *Martin Buber: The Life of
Dialogue* (The Chicago University Press, 1955), p. 20.

[4] *Nature and Values* (Henry Holt & Company, Inc., 1945),
p. 62.

[5] *Nature, Man and God,* p. 211.

[6] *Christianity in Thought and Action* (The Macmillan
Company, 1936), p. 26.

[7] *Ethics,* pp. 55–62.

he had to leave his ethic "half-baked" because of his early death and the privation of his heroic last years.

Hence it follows that in Christian situation ethics nothing is worth anything in and of itself. It gains or acquires its value only because it happens to help persons (thus being good) or to hurt persons (thus being bad). The person who is "finding" the value may be either divine (God willing the good) or human (a man valuing something). Persons—God, self, neighbor—are both the subjects and the objects of value; *they* determine it to be value, and they determine it to be value for some person's sake. It is a value because somebody decided it was worth something. Oscar Wilde was clever but not deep when he said, "A cynic is a man who knows the price of everything, and the value of nothing." There is no other way to set value but by price, even though *money* is not always the truest measure. Good and evil are extrinsic to the thing or the action. It all depends on the situation. What is right in one case, e.g., lending cash to a father who needs it for his hungry family, may be wrong in another case, e.g., lending cash to a father with hungry children when he is known to be a compulsive gambler or alcoholic.

Speaking more timidly than a situationist would, but solidly on the point, Temple says: "It is doubtful if any act is right 'in itself.' Every act is a link in a chain of causes and effects. It cannot be said that it is wrong to take away a man's possessions against his will, for that would condemn all taxation—or the removal of a revolver from a homicidal maniac; neither of these is stealing—which is always wrong; though high authority has held that a starving man may steal a loaf rather than die of hunger, because life is of more value than property and should be chosen first for preservation if both cannot be preserved together. The rightness of an act, then, nearly always and perhaps always, depends on the way in which the act is related to circumstances; this is what is meant by calling it relatively right; but this does not in the least imply that it is only doubtfully right. It may be, in those circumstances, certainly and absolutely right."[8]

LOVE IS A PREDICATE

Apart from the helping or hurting of people, ethical judgments or evaluations are meaningless. Having as its supreme norm the neighbor love commanded of Christians, Christian situation ethics asserts firmly and definitely: *Value, worth, ethical quality, goodness or badness, right or wrong—these things are only predicates, they are not properties.* They are not "given" or objectively "real" or self-existent.[9] There is only one thing that is always good and right, intrinsically good regardless of the context, and that one thing is love. Yet we should not, perhaps, call love a "thing." Neutral as it is as a word, it may tend in the reader's mind to reify love, to suggest that it is a tangible, objective existent. (The New Testament sometimes speaks of love as if it were a property, sometimes as a predicate. Paul and the Gospel writers were entirely innocent of the problem we are discussing. It never occurred to them.)

But love is not a substantive—nothing of the kind. It is a principle, a "formal" principle, expressing what type of real actions Christians are to call good. (Exactly the same is true of justice.) It is the *only* principle that always obliges us in conscience. Unlike all other principles you might mention, love alone when well served is always good and right in every situation. Love is the only univer-

[8] *Religious Experience* (London: James Clarke & Company, Ltd., 1958), pp. 173–174.

[9] A philosophical defense of the predicative concept is in Stephen Toulmin, *An Examination of the Place of Reason in Ethics* (Cambridge: Cambridge University Press, 1950). He successfully attacks the "nonnatural" property thesis of G. E. Moore.

sal. But love is not something we *have* or *are,* it is something we *do.* Our task is to act so that more good (i.e., loving-kindness) will occur than any possible alternatives; we are to be "optimific," to seek an optimum of loving-kindness. It is an attitude, a disposition, a leaning, a preference, a purpose.

When we say that love is always good, what we mean is that whatever is loving in any *particular* situation is good! Love is a way of relating to persons, and of using things. As H. R. Niebuhr once said, "God nowhere commands love for its own sake."[10] It is for the sake of people and it is not a good-in-itself. Neither, of course, is it merely one "virtue" among others, as some pious moral manuals and Sunday school tracts make it out to be. It is not a virtue at all; it is the one and only *regulative principle* of Christian ethics.

Reinhold Niebuhr, who is closer to situationism than to any other ethical method, nevertheless held a sort of supernaturalistic notion of love as some "thing" or power that men lack except in a finite and insufficient measure. He saw love as an "absolute" property or capacity or state, rather than a predicate, a way of characterizing what we *do* when we actually *act* in a concrete situation. He spoke of love as something we *have* in one measure or another.

Therefore he could hold that Jesus' cross typified a "perfect love" which was unique, utter sacrificial unselfishness, beyond men except as approximated in relative justice.[11] On the contrary, if love is to be understood situationally, as a predicate rather than a property, what we must understand is that Jesus' going to the cross was

[10] *Christ and Culture* (Harper & Brothers, 1951), p. 15.
[11] *An Interpretation of Christian Ethics* (Harper & Brothers, 1935), passim. In 1956 he said, "I am not . . . able to defend, or interested in defending, any position I took [in that book]" (*Reinhold Niebuhr,* ed. by C. W. Kegley and R. W. Bretall [The Macmillan Company, 1956], p. 435).

his role and vocation in *his* situation with *his* obligation
as the Son of God. We cannot therefore speak with Niebuhr of the "impossibility" of love, even though we join
him in speaking of its *relativity*. Love does not say to us,
"*Be* like me." It says, "*Do* what you can where you are."

Karl Barth puts himself in an untenable corner with
the intrinsic fallacy. On the subject of abortion he first
says that an unformed, unborn embryo is a child and that
to stop it is murder. Then he declares, uncomfortably, that
although abortion is "absolutely" wrong, it can sometimes
be excused and forgiven. Therefore he is in the intrinsic
camp but merciful about it. Finally he blurts out: "Let us
be quite frank and say that there are situations in which
the killing of germinating life does not constitute murder
but is in fact commanded" (italics added).[12] This puts
Barth in the anomalous position of saying that to obey
God's command (to act lovingly) is to do something absolutely wrong. Clearly this is theological-ethical nonsense.
(It undermines his treatment of euthanasia, sterlization,
and other questions for the same reason.)

Barth might have trusted Luther more. Said Luther:
"Therefore, when the law impels one against love, it ceases
and should *no longer be a law;* but where no obstacle is in
the way, the keeping of the law is a proof of love, which
lies hidden in the heart. Therefore you have need of the
law, that love may be manifested; but if it cannot be kept
without injury to the neighbor, God wants us to suspend
and ignore the law."[13]

Only in the divine being, only in God, is love substantive. With men it is a formal principle, a predicate.
Only with God is it a property. This is because God *is*
love. Men, who are finite, only *do* love. That is, they try in

[12] *Church Dogmatics,* Vol. III, Bk. 4, pp. 416–421.
[13] Sermon, Eighteenth Sunday After Trinity, in "The
Church Postil," *Works,* ed. by J. N. Linker (Luther House,
1905), Vol. V, p. 175.

obedience to obey love's command to be like God, to imitate him. The *imitatio Dei, imitatio Christi,* is to love the neighbor. Says Augustine, in order to know whether a man is a *good* man "one does not ask what he believes or what he hopes, but what he loves."[14] Love may only be "predicated" of human actions and relationships according to how they take shape in the situation. Men may be lovable and loving, but only God *is* love. And in the Bible the image of God, man's model, is not reason but love. "God is not reason but love, and he employs reason as the instrument of his love."[15] In the strict sense of the word, this is the theology of situation ethics.

The other side of the proposition that only love is intrinsically good is, of course, that only malice is intrinsically evil. If goodwill is the only thing we are always obliged to do, then ill will is the only thing we are always forbidden to do. A literal synonym for goodwill is "benevolence," but by usage the word now smacks of something far less intense and committed than the *agapē* of the New Testament! Even "goodwill" has acquired a connotation of *respectability,* as when it is paid for as an asset in the sale of a business.

The opposite of benevolence is "malevolence," but here again the word's use has given it a more direct and deliberate meaning than Christian situation ethics cares to adopt. Indeed, in any careful analysis it must be made quite clear that actually the true opposite of love is not hate but indifference. Hate, bad as it is, at least treats the neighbor as a *thou,* whereas indifference turns the neighbor into an *it,* a thing. This is why we may say that there is actually one thing worse than evil itself, and that is indifference to evil. In human relations the nadir of

[14] "Enchiridion," Ch. 117, in *Works,* ed. by M. Dods (Edinburgh: T. & T. Clark, 1873), Vol. IX, p. 256.
[15] Martin Heinecken, *God in the Space Age* (Holt, Rinehart & Winston, Inc., 1959), p. 168.

morality, the lowest point, as far as Christian ethics is concerned, is manifest in the phrase, "I couldn't care less." This is why we must not forget that the New Testament calls upon us to love people, not principles.

Kant's second maxim, to treat people as ends and never as means, is strictly parallel to the New Testament's "law of love." (The term actually never occurs, *ho nomos teis agapeis*, but it is substantially there in such passages as Rom. 13:10 and Gal. 5:14.) And Kant's contention that the only really good thing is a good will, which is what the New Testament means by *agapē* or "love," goes necessarily and logically with his second maxim. Whatever is benevolent is right; whatever is malevolent or indifferent is wrong. This is the radical simplicity of the Gospel's ethic, even though it can lead situationally to the most complicated, headaching, heartbreaking calculations and gray rather than black or white decisions.

ONLY EXTRINSIC

This posture or perspective sets us over against all "intrinsicalist" ethics, against all "given" or "natural" or "objectively valid" laws and maxims, whether of the natural law or the Scriptural law varieties. It means, too, that there are no universals of any kind. Only love is objectively valid, only love is universal. Therefore when John Bennett pleads, in the spirit of Luther's *pecca fortiter*, that "there are situations in which the best we can do is evil," we have to oppose what he says—much as we admire its spirit.[16] On Bennett's basis, if a small neighborhood merchant tells a lie to divert some "protection" racketeers from their victims, no matter how compassionately the lie is told, he has chosen to do *evil*. It is, of course, excused

[16] *Christianity and the Contemporary Scene*, ed. by R. C. Miller and H. M. Shires (Morehouse-Gorman Company, Inc., 1942), p. 119.

or forgiven or pardoned as a so-called "lesser evil." This has always been possible in the merciful casuistry of the ethical realists or intrinsicalists. But no matter how lovingly such "bad things" may be done they are still evil, still wrong, they still require repentance and forgiveness!

This confused assertion that the shopkeeper's lie is both loving and wrong is an obvious contradiction. It is due to the intrinsic doctrine of value. Because its starting point is an ontological rather than existential conception of right and wrong, it is compelled in this barbarous way to divorce what is right from what is good. It even opposes them to each other! (This is what the Texas rancher recognized in *The Rainmaker*, already mentioned in our Foreword.) It causes, and always has caused, Christian ethicists to claim that what love requires is often not the "right" thing but nevertheless excusable because of conditions. But for the situationist what makes the lie right is its loving purpose; he is not hypnotized by some abstract law, "Thou shalt not lie." He refuses to evaluate "white lies" told out of pity and espionage in wartime as *ipso jure* wrong.

If a lie is told unlovingly it is wrong, evil; if it is told in love it is good, right. Kant's legalism produced a "universal"—that a lie is always wrong. But what if you have to tell a lie to keep a promised secret? Maybe you lie, and if so, good for you if you follow love's lead. Paul's "speaking the truth in love" (Eph. 4:15) illuminates the point: we are to tell the truth for love's sake, not for its own sake. If love vetoes the truth, so be it. Right and wrong, good and bad, are things that *happen* to what we say and do, whether they are "veracious" or not, depending upon how much love is served in the situation. The merchant chose to do a good thing, not an excusably bad thing. Love *made* it good. *The situationist holds that whatever is the most loving thing in the situation is the right and good thing.* It is not excusably evil, it is positively good. This is the fundamental point of the extrinsic position.

The intrinsicalists, i.e., the legalists, have always domi-
nated Christian ethics. "It is," says Brunner, "the curse of
'Christian morality' that it always regards the most legalistic view as the 'most serious.' "[17] It is obvious to some
of us at least that the positive, extrinsic view has never
really even been glimpsed by them. They have therefore
had, under the pressure of love, to develop the Lesser Evil
(or its other side, the Greater Good). The backbone of all
legalism is the notion that value (good or evil) is a property "in" our actions. The sway of this metaphysics in
moral theology has forced such absurd positions as this:
A captured soldier may not commit suicide out of sacrificial love, under overweening torture, to avoid betraying
his comrades to the enemy; this is because of the evil of
suicide itself, intrinsically.[18]

Bishop Pike tries to be a consistent situationist. He sets
"existential" ethics over against "ontological" ethics in a
very promising way. But it never really comes off! He says
stoutly, "As St. Thomas Aquinas reminded us, a negative
particular destroys an affirmative universal."[19] He says
this in pointing out that even in the Apocrypha, Judith is
praised for lying to Holofernes and using her sex (though
she remained a *technical* virgin, according to the canonical
story) whoringly in order to murder him. Yet for all this
sturdy ethical evaluation of Judith's situational action "to
save Israel," Pike ends with the opinion that a justifiable
violation of a sound principle (e.g., homicide is wrong)
is never *good*, however "right" situationally!

He cannot disentangle himself from the intrinsicalists'
net. He *thinks* of right and wrong as real things, "onto-
logically," after all. He says, "What we have is not an
exception to the rules which makes [the action] *good* or

[17] *The Divine Imperative,* p. 355.
[18] See *The Clergy Review,* Vol. 40 (1955), pp. 170–174,
534–537.
[19] *Doing the Truth,* pp. 40–42, 142.

even neutral in character, but a balance of goods and evils and a resulting choice of the greater of two goods, the lesser of two evils (though . . . the choice may be, in the situation, *the right thing*)" (his italics). This is the talk of ontological or intrinsic ethics, not of existential or extrinsic ethics!

But situation ethics, on the extrinsic view that right and wrong are only predicates, not properties, finds the locus of value in the circumstances of the soldier's suicide, and in what it means for people. It locates the evil in the multiple destruction of life and the betrayal of loyalty that results if the prisoner's willing sacrifice of his life, like Christ's on the cross, is forbidden by a law or principle. Extrinsicalism fights back at the unlovingness of law-bound conscience which reifies good and evil, treating value as if it were a thing-in-itself (Kant's *Ding-an-sich*), when in fact it is only a function of human decisions. Here is the normative relativism we espouse. It waves good-by to legalism and dogmatism.

For the classical moralists, therefore, suicide and lying are always wrong regardless of circumstances and relativities, even though loving concern might excuse such actions in the situation. Faced with the shocking possibility that law may have to condemn what love has done, the priests and preachers have worked out a false kind of casuistry that has grown up into a bewildering thicket of pilpul. Confused and contradictory and muddled as it is, it is after all a loving attempt to escape entrapment in its own metaphysic. It has to lie on a Procrustean bed of its own making. Having set out laws based on ethical absolutes and universals, love compels them to make more and more rules with which to break the rules. This is the ridiculous result when law ethics (as in the Christian tradition) tries to keep control, yet wants also to pay homage to love. It can't eat its cake and have it too.

But it is all wrong at the very start: the intrinsic theory

of goodness is what the Greeks called the *prōton pseudon* —the basic mistake of the legalists. No law or principle or value is good as such—not life or truth or chastity or property or marriage or anything but love. *Only one thing is intrinsically good, namely, love: nothing else at all.*

IV

Love Is the Only Norm

*The Second Proposition: "The ruling norm of
Christian decision is love: nothing else."*

LOVE IS, AS we have said, a monolithic and jealous standard, a univalent norm. It shoulders aside all other, lesser
goods. Christian situation ethics reduces law from a statutory system of rules to the love canon alone. For this
reason, Jesus was ready without hesitation to ignore the
obligations of Sabbath observance, to do forbidden work
on the seventh day. "The sabbath was made for man"
(Mark 2: 27–28). In exactly the same way Paul could
eat his food kosher or not, simply depending on whether
in any situation it is edifying (upbuilding) for others
(I Cor. 10: 23–26).

LOVE REPLACES LAW

Jesus and Paul replaced the precepts of Torah with the
living principle of *agapē*—*agapē* being *goodwill at work
in partnership with reason.* It seeks the neighbor's best
interest with a careful eye to all the factors in the situation. They redeemed law from the letter that kills and
brought it back to the spirit that gives it life. And to do
this, law and general rules always have to be refined *back*
from legalistic prescriptions and from rabbinical pilpul to

the heart principle of love. This was indeed a collision
between two ways of being good, as far as Pharisaism and
Jesus were concerned. (We do not ignore the fact that the
Sifra on Lev. 19:18 is, "Rabbi Akiba said: 'The supreme
and inclusive norm—*kalol gadol*—of the Law is this:
Thou shalt love thy neighbor as thyself.' ") We follow
law, *if at all,* for love's sake; we do not follow love for
law's sake.

We must be quite adamant about this. The conventional view is that through obeying law we serve love,
because (it is claimed) there is no real conflict at all between law and love. Even Brunner comes too close to
saying this, in explaining Luther's teaching that law serves
love threefoldly as discipline, repentance, and guidance.[1]

Often we hear quoted the Judaizing phrase in Matt.
5: 17–20 (and Luke 16:17), "Not an iota, not a dot,
will pass from the law," and "Whoever relaxes one of the
least of these commandments" shall be small potatoes in
the Kingdom. Literalizers or fundamentalists take these
phrases, however inconsistent they are with the rest of the
Gospels and with Paul's letters, as a law requiring the law!
Bernhard Häring, C.Ss.R., makes an impressive effort to
ease the law ethic by pleading the primacy of love over
law, but at bottom he still identifies law with love, and
when he stresses the spirit rather than the letter of the
law, he is still distinguishing them, not *separating* them as
a situationist would.[2] The love commandment (the Shema
of Deut. 6:4–5 combined with Lev. 19:18, in Mark
12:29–32, etc.) is, so runs the argument, Jesus' summary of the *law!*

But here lies the issue. Is the Summary to be taken as a
compendium or as a distillation? Legalists take it as a

[1] *The Divine Imperative,* pp. 140–151.
[2] *Christian Renewal in a Changing World* (Desclee Co.,
Inc., 1964), p. 19, and *The Law of Christ,* 2 vols. (The
Newman Press, 1961 and 1963).

compendium, as a collection and conflation of many laws, obedience to all of them being implicit in their coming together as a summary. Situationists, however, take it to mean a distillation, i.e., that the essential spirit and ethos of many laws has been distilled or liberated, extracted, filtered out, with the legal husks, or rubbish, thrown away as dross.

The situationist replies to all claims that love commands us to follow the law, "Yes, all right. We are willing to follow principles and precepts *if* they serve love, *when* they do. But just the same, there can be and often is a conflict between love and law." They cannot be partners; at best, love only employs law when it seems worthwhile.

Let's look at the Ten Commandments, Ex. 20:2–17 and Deut. 5:6–21, for instance. They are very "sacred" in popular Judaism and Christianity, and much pious lip service is paid them even in secular culture. Protestants regard them as God's positive revealed enactments, and Catholics regard them as natural laws discernible by reason but backed up by specific revelation via Moses' tablets of stone. We shall refer to them in the numbering of their order in the Exodus text.

TABLETS OF STONE

The first one is: "I am the Lord your God, you shall have no other gods before [but?] me." This causes situation ethics no difficulty. "Aha," say the legalists, "how can you get around *that* one?" The situationist has no wish to get around it for two obvious reasons. (1) It is only a "law" in the sense that we can speak of the "law of love" or the "law of one's being." It is a tautology, not a true commandment. One does not worship idols, i.e., other gods, if one does not. It only says (to primitive Semitic henotheists) that if you have faith in one God, you won't have faith in any other! It only states a fact, a "fact of faith." It is an indicative, not an imperative. Monotheism cannot be commanded.

Furthermore, (2) one could surely *pretend* to have no faith in God, or in any combination of gods, if it were necessary for loving cause. We could make a formal but false apostasy under persecution for the sake of dependents or the life of an illegal underground church. If the First Commandment is meant to prohibit atheistic or non-Yahwistic declarations, then it becomes like other laws and can be broken for love's sake. God knows the secrets of the heart; he knows when he is denied falsely and lovingly, and he also knows when he is acclaimed falsely and unlovingly.

As to the second prohibition, "You shall not make for yourself a graven image . . . of anything," if it is taken to be a prohibition of idolatry, love might technically, i.e., in a false way, violate it as it might violate the first prohibition. If it commands aniconic worship (no images), Catholic and Eastern Christians have always broken the law! Jesus is constantly shown in Christian worship, even though God as transcendent escapes being depicted. And there is some evidence that the Jews themselves used sacred images, even under Moses. (A Mowinckel says they did, an Eichrodt says they did not!) If it means there is to be no pictorial art at all (sculpture, painting, photography), as many strict Jews have interpreted it to the impoverishment of their culture, then we might reasonably and lovingly say it is a *bad* law indeed. Who would disagree?

The third item in the Decalogue, "You shall not take the name of the Lord your God in vain," presents exegetical problems but no ethical difficulty. Does it mean we must not take solemn oaths? If so, we all rightly violate it in court or, for example, as clergy do in being ordained. (They are violating in addition the injunction of the Sermon on the Mount, Matt. 5:34, 37: "Do not swear

at all. . . . Let what you say be simply 'Yes' or 'No.' ")
If it merely prohibits using the divine name for magical
purposes or false oath-taking or irreverent expletives
(swearing in that sense), we ought to obey it *unless some
real good can be gained by violating it.*

Jeanie Deans in Sir Walter Scott's novel *The Heart of
Midlothian* was faced with the question whether she
would tell a lie at her sister Effie's trial for the murder of
her bastard child. She was innocent, as Jeanie well knew,
but there was no honest way to rescue her from a false
tissue of circumstantial evidence. Jeanie was torn terribly
between her loving concern and her Calvinist legalism!
K. E. Kirk once remarked blandly and piously, "We may
doubt whether any serious-minded Christian could really
have advised Jeanie to lie in cold blood," adding that we
can feel the claims of sympathy for Effie in her danger
but "an even greater claim is that of Jeanie's soul."[3] Here,
clearly, is the temper of soft legalism, i.e., soft on the
surface but hard as flint underneath.

The fourth of these laws, "Remember the sabbath day.
. . . In it you shall do no work," is of course completely
overthrown by Christians who make Sunday, the first day
of the week, the Lord's Day, rather than the Old Testament's Sabbath or seventh day, Saturday. We still have
a lot of Sabbatarians who like to make "the Lord's Day"
a day of doom and gloom. But few even pretend to obey
this prohibition of Sunday work. Who could or would in
an interdependent society like ours, in which goods and
services must and should be produced on Saturdays and
Sundays? And why not, anyway? The situationist says
not, "The better the day, the better the deed," but, "The
better the deed, the better the day."

The last six of the commandments, for filial piety
(Honor your parents), and against killing (or is it murder?), adultery, stealing, false witness, and covetousness,

[3] *Conscience and Its Problems*, pp. 351–352.

are more "ethical" in the ordinary nontheological use of
the word. All but the fifth (Honor your father and
mother) are universal negatives. But situation ethics has
good reason to hold it as a *duty* in some situations to break
them, *any or all of them*. We would be better advised and
better off to drop the legalist's love of law, and accept only
the law of love. This solitary "law" is the Summary, understood as a successor to the commandments and not a com-
pressor. (This is the point of Bornkamm's treatment of
Mark 7:15, which tells how Jesus directly threw out all
the "religious" dietary laws.[4] "There is nothing outside a
man which by going into him can defile him." We can
paraphrase Jesus and extend his logic: "There is nothing
outside a situation which by going into it can prejudge it.")

Bonhoeffer in his *Ethics* (p. 116) turns the maxim
that killing is wrong into an absolute prohibition. That is,
he makes it another norm alongside love! "All deliberate
killing of innocent life is arbitrary," he says, and whatever
is "arbitrary" is in his view wrong. He adumbrates this
law from an examination of the ethics of euthanasia. But
what then of Mother Maria's suicide (euthanasia is one
form of suicide) in the Nazi concentration camp at Bel-
sen? She chose to die in a gas chamber in the stead of a
young ex-Jewish girl Communist. The Gestapo had arrested her in a Paris suburb for running an underground
escape route for Jews. The girl survived the war and became a Christian. Mother Maria sacrificed her life on the
"model" of Christ, and Bonhoeffer, who also died bravely
at the Nazis' hands, would have loved her for it. Yet, ab-
surdly, he had to invoke a rival law that says her love
cannot follow her Master's example *too closely!*

Incidentally, like Barth and many others, Bonhoeffer
absolutized the general rule against killing one's self or
others without ever facing the fact that to denounce

[4] Günther Bornkamm, *Jesus of Nazareth* (Harper &
Brothers, 1960), p. 98.

"murder" is a very question-begging universal negative. It really means "immoral killing is immoral." It begs the whole question whether killing is ever possibly right. Bonhoeffer admits that in self-defense and war and capital punishment killing is moral because the victim in those cases is not "innocent." The Sixth Commandment of Moses is rendered as "Thou shalt not kill," but obviously the Jews killed for food, punishment, and war. It should be, "Thou shalt do no murder"—i.e., *unlawful* killing. No art is more skillfully adept at the use of weasel words than law. It has to be, because it is what it is—an attempt to absolutize the relative.

A situationist might or might not agree on particular exceptions like capital punishment, but he would be sure to protest that, in principle, even killing "innocent" people might be right. Mother Maria, for example, who killed herself. What of Bonhoeffer's own decision that Hitler was not innocent and should be assassinated? Would he actually have turned his back on a man caught hopelessly in the burning wreckage of a plane, who begged to be shot?

NEITHER NATURE NOR SCRIPTURE

Christian ethics is not in truth and cannot long remain in appearance a systematized scheme of codified conduct. Every religious legalism, whether of the Catholic natural law variety or of the Protestant Scriptural law variety, is sooner or later repudiated. It is overcome by the spirit of Paul's insistence that what matters is not what is lawful but what is upbuilding. It is sub-Christian to imagine that the juridical order ever exactly, or even often, coincides with the moral order.

Legalism is legalism whether it rests upon nature or upon Scripture. Both kinds are quicksand. Lindsay Dewar has pointed out recently, trying to preserve the idea of natural law, that even though "there be doubt as to what

are the agreed principles of the Natural Law—and the
doubt has been magnified by some writers recently[5]—
there is, to say the least, no less doubt as to the exact
interpretation of the Sermon [on the Mount]."[6] Exactly so.
Both are in the same bad fix.

To those in the natural law camp we say, "Oh, yes.
You may postulate the presence of right and wrong objectively in the nature of things, *de rerum natura*. But
this does not entitle you to suppose that you can *possess*
them cognitively—that you can know what right and
wrong are and wrap them up neatly in formulas, thinking
God's thoughts after him." No twentieth-century man of
even average training will turn his back on the anthro-
pological and psychological evidence for relativity in
morals.[7] There are no "universal laws" held by all men
everywhere at all times, no consensus of all men. Any
precepts all men can agree to are platitudes such as "do
the good and avoid the evil" or "to each according to his
due." What *is* good, when and how, and what *is* due, is
always widely debated in theory and hotly debated in
concrete cases.

Besides this, the attempt to study nature and discern
God's will in it is only a hoary old sample of the "natural-
istic fallacy" of deriving *ought* from *is,* already referred to.
A federal judge a year or so before the school integration
decision of the Supreme Court in 1954 upheld the right,

[5] Especially those who support the new morality or situation ethics.

[6] *Moral Theology in the Modern World* (London: A. R.
Mowbray & Company, Ltd., 1964), p. 44.

[7] A less pretentious, more attractive notion is John Bennett's
"common ground morality." It expresses the same hunger for
universals but grounds them in cultural constants, not in
nature or reality. Cf. "Christian Ethics and the National
Conscience," Bell Lecture No. 6 (Boston University, 1965),
pp. 13–18.

as "a" right, of a city to segregate its golf course on the natural law ground that birds of different kinds do not rest on the same limb of the tree.

Cicero, in his *De legibus,* I.17, 45, said seriously, "Only a madman could maintain that the distinction between the honorable and the dishonorable, between virtue and vice, is a matter of opinion, not of nature." This is nevertheless precisely and exactly what situation ethics maintains.

To those in the Scriptural law camp we can say, "Oh, yes. You may sincerely believe that 'Holy Writ' is the 'Word of God.' But if you try to literalize the ethical sayings in it, you will soon find yourself in lots worse trouble than the mere headache of trying to figure out what some sayings mean ('Render therefore to Caesar the things that are Caesar's, and to God the things that are God's') or how to figure out what to do when you turn its maxims into rules ('Do not resist one who is evil')." Either cheap melancholy or utter frustration will follow if we turn the Bible into a rules book, forgetting that an editorial collection of scattered sayings, such as the Sermon on the Mount, offers us at the most some paradigms or suggestions. Only the Summary of the Law is the law! Brunner is quite right: *"None* of the commandments in the Sermon on the Mount are to be understood as laws, so that those who hear them can go away feeling, 'Now I know what I have to do!' "[8]

LOVE HAS NO EQUALS

In its very marrow Christian ethics is a situation ethic. The new morality, the emerging contemporary Christian conscience, separates Christian conduct from rigid creeds and rigid codes. Some of its critics, both Protestant and Catholic, seem to fear that by dropping codes it will drop

[8] *The Divine Imperative,* p. 136.

its Christian commitment.[9] What it does is to treat all rules and principles and "virtues" (that is to say, all "universals") as love's servants and subordinates, to be quickly kicked out of the house if they forget their place and try to take over. Ayn Rand, the egoist and jungle-ethic writer, tersely describes the love ethic (except that it does not teach us to *scorn* a whore, only to help and redeem her): "A morality which teaches you to scorn a whore who gives her body indiscriminately to all men—this same morality demands that you surrender your soul to promiscuous love for all comers."[10]

Augustine was right to make love the source principle, the hinge principle upon which all other "virtues" hang, whether "cardinal" (natural) or "theological" (revealed). Love is not one virtue among others, one principle among equals, not even a *primus inter pares*. One theologian, Robert Gleason, S.J., in a full-dress attack on situation ethics, threw down the gauntlet most lucidly (and how different a challenge from that of Ayn Rand!) by asserting, "While the motive of love is a noble one, it is not in Christian tradition to present it as the exclusive motive for moral action."[11] This succinctly challenges the view that love has a monopoly control. It flies directly in the face of Paul's "single saying" in Gal. 5:14 and the conclusion of his hymn to love, I Cor., ch. 13. But what else can the man of law do, trapped as he is in his intrinsic rights and wrongs and his collections and systems of virtues and absolutes?

To illustrate what legalism does in the civil order, we might recall what happened a few years ago in an English

[9] C. B. Eavey, *Principles of Christian Ethics* (Zondervan Publishing House, 1958), p. 246; Kenneth Moore, O. Carm., *American Ecclesiastical Review,* Vol. 135 (1956), pp. 29–38.

[10] *Atlas Shrugged* (Random House, Inc., 1957), p. 1033.

[11] "Situational Morality," *Thought,* Vol. 32 (1957), pp. 533–558.

court. The law reads that a marriage must be validated
("consummated") by sexual union. In the case before it,
it found that a young wife had conceived a son by means
of A.I.H. (artificial insemination from her husband) because he was suffering a temporary erectile failure, subsequently corrected. The court was faithful to its law and
ruled that the little boy was conceived out of wedlock, i.e.,
that the child was a bastard, the mother an adulteress or
fornicator, the wife husbandless when her child was born,
the father without a son and heir, and the child an outlaw.
All of this even though their child was seed of their seed,
flesh of their flesh!

Augustine was right again, as situationists see it, to
reduce the whole Christian ethic to the single maxim,
Dilige et quod vis, fac (Love with care and *then* what you
will, do). It was not, by the way, *Ama et fac quod vis*
(Love with desire and do what you please)![12] It was not
antinomianism.

Christian love is not desire. *Agapē* is giving love—non-
reciprocal, neighbor-regarding—"neighbor" meaning "everybody," even an enemy (Luke 6:32–35). It is usually
distinguished from friendship love (*philia*) and romantic
love (*erōs*), both of which are selective and exclusive.
Erotic love and philic love have their proper place in our
human affairs but they are not what is meant by *agapē*,
agapeic love or "Christian love." Erotic and philic love are
emotional, but the effective principle of Christian love is
will, disposition; it is an *attitude*, not feeling.

Situationists welcome the German label for this conception, *Gesinnungs-ethik*, an attitudinal ethic rather than
a legal one. "Have this mind among yourselves, which
you have in Christ Jesus" (Phil. 2:5), and *then*, as
Augustine says, whatever you do will be right! The mind

---

[12] *Ep. Joan.*, vii. 5, in J. P. Migne, *Patralogiae cursus com-
pletus, series Latina* (Paris: Garnier Fr., 1864), Vol. 35,
col. 2033. *"Semel ergo breve praeceptum tibi praecipitur,
Dilige, et quod vis fac."*

of him whom Bonhoeffer called "the Man for others" is
to be for others, for neighbors. *That* is *agapē*.

What a difference it makes when love, understood
agapeically, is boss; when love is the only norm. How free
and therefore responsible we are! The natural law moralists, just to cite an example of legalism, are trapped into
cheating on love or even into altogether denying love's
demands, in the matter of sterilizations. In the name of
a "natural law" of procreation they have to prohibit ob-
stetricians from tying off the tubes of a cardiac mother in
delivery, for whom another pregnancy is a mortal danger.
In the name of a "natural law" of secrecy they have been
known to admonish a doctor to withhold from an innocent girl the fact that she is about to marry a syphilitic
man. No such cut-and-dried, coldly predetermined (prej-
udiced) position could or would be taken by a situationist.

At this juncture we might do well to look at the question whether a situationist can agree with legalism's effort
to *force* people to be good. The answer is, of course, that
"it all depends." It seems impossible to see any sound
reason for most of such attempts to legislate morality.
Yet there was a lot of furious surprise in a California city
recently when the police found a wife-swapping club and
learned there were no *laws* to stop it. The District Attorney saw no cause to be alarmed, even so. "Wife-swapping
just doesn't violate any section of the penal code." It is
doubtful that love's cause is helped by any of the sex
laws that try to dictate sexual practices for consenting
adults.

The triple terrors of infection, conception, and detec-
tion, which once scared people into "Christian" sex relations (marital monopoly), have pretty well become ob-
solete through medicine and urbanism. There is less and
less cause, on the basis of situation ethics, for the opinion
that people should abide by, or pretend to, an ideal or
standard that is not their own. It may well be, especially

with the young, that situationists should advise continence or chastity for practical expedient reasons, but that is a situational, not a legalistic approach.

OBJECTIONS

A common objection to situation ethics is that it calls for more critical intelligence, more factual information, and more self-starting commitment to righteousness than most people can bring to bear. We all know the army veteran who "wishes the war was back" because he could tell the good guys from the bad guys by the uniforms they wore. There are those who say situationism ignores the reality of human sin or egocentricity, and fails to appreciate the finitude of human reason.

People who think there was literally once a "Fall" (they abound in church circles) would say that law is needed now to control us, echoing Paul's famous discourse on law in Gal. 3:19 to 4:7, especially his thesis that law acts as a custodian, judging us until Christ comes, until we throw ourselves upon God's grace (i.e., the power of God's love). But Paul proceeded to say, "For freedom Christ *has* set us free; stand fast therefore, and do not submit again to a yoke of slavery [i.e., law]" (Gal. 5:1). This might well be the slogan of Christian situation ethics.

It reminds us of the Legend of the Grand Inquisitor in Dostoevsky's novel *The Brothers Karamazov*.[13] It is Ivan's story to Alyosha about the terrible burden of freedom. Christ returned to earth, and the Spanish Inquisitor, recognizing him in the crowd watching a religious procession, had him arrested at once. In the dead of night he visited the Christ in secret, embarrassed, trying to explain that most people do not want freedom, they want security. If you really love people, he argued, you make them happy,

[13] See Modern Library Edition (Random House, Inc., 1955), pp. 292–309.

not free. Freedom is danger, openness. They want law, not responsibility; they want the neurotic comfort of rules, not the spiritual open places of decision-making. They prefer absolutes to relativities. The Christ, he says, must not come back to start again all of that old business about freedom and grace and commitment and responsibility. Let things be, just let the church (the law) handle them. Let him please go away.

Psychologically, the Inquisitor's plea is suited to many people. But there are a lot it does not fit. People are, in any case, going to have to grow up into situation ethics, no doubt of it. The Christian is called to be mature, to live by grace and freedom, to *respond* to life, to be responsible. This is the vocation of all situationists, most certainly the "calling" of Christian situationists. The motive and purpose behind law, however hidden it may be, is to *minimize obligation*, to make it clear exactly how much you must do *and no more*. Grace, on the other hand, refuses to put a ceiling or a floor on concern for the neighbor. Love, unlike law, sets no carefully calculated limits on obligation; it seeks the most good possible in every situation. It maximizes or optimizes obligation.

When a woman is viciously attacked, fifty neighbors watch without helping, without even calling the police. A farmer destroys his barn to keep a fire from spreading to his neighbor's property, but the neighbor won't help to compensate the farmer. An indifferent passer-by watches a baby drown. A motorist sees a wheel wobbling loose on the car in front of him but merely slows down to keep out of the way of a pileup. American and English law on principle do not have a "good Samaritan" provision (Germany, Italy, the Soviet Union, France, do). The Anglo-American principle is "Mind your own business"; the law limits your obligation, you are responsible only for what you do—not for what you should or could have done. This is the prudence of self-centeredness and indifference, contrasted to the aggressive, questing prudence of *agapē*.

Law may be indeed a necessary feature of community and *can* even be constructive. But when the motive of the law observer is to hide behind the letter of the law in order to escape the higher demands of its spirit or to escape the complexities of responsible decision, that is cheap legalism. An example is a canon of the Episcopal Church which, believe it or not, from 1868 to 1946 gave the right of remarriage only to the "innocent" party to a civil divorce.[14] (Everybody knows that the courts employ utterly dishonest and false, conventional pleas in such cases, so that only too often the legally "innocent" are the morally guilty.)

Massachusetts has a law under which, in collisions at intersections, the car struck from behind by the other's bumper is the aggrieved party. This evades the situation facts and only encourages drivers to race to intersections to get their noses out first in case of trouble! If Brunner is right, as quoted earlier, that people regard legalism as the most "serious" morality, the point of view of this book is that it is not anything of the sort; that in truth it only too often evades the depth, competence, and responsibility of free decision.

Absolute negatives and absolute affirmatives alike have this neurotic character of falsifying complex realities. Albert Schweitzer is quite right to say that "the good conscience is an invention of the devil."[15] Classical pacifism is an example; it holds the use of violence to be always wrong regardless of the situation. This is a legalism, even though many pacifists would be unhappy to think of it as such. The subtlety here is this: the pacifist knows that if, as in the "just war" doctrine, it is possible that some wars are just and some are not, the pacifist with his absolute prohibition is bound to be ethically right some of the time,

[14] See D. B. Stevick, *Canon Law* (The Seabury Press, Inc., 1965), pp. 158–159.
[15] Quoted in J. A. Davidson, *A New Look at Morals* (Toronto: Ryerson Press, 1964), p. 21.

whereas the situationist could be wrong *every* time, failing to recognize when a war is just and trying to justify one when it is not justifiable. The pacifist is safe ethically in a way, as all legalists are, whereas the situationist is always vulnerable to error in any decision-making situation. Nevertheless, we must favor a casuistry in which every man is his own casuist when the decision-making chips are down. Decision is "a risk rooted in the courage of being" free.[16]

A noteworthy complaint is that situation ethics presumes more ability to know the facts and weigh them than most people can muster. It is true that all of us are limited in how much we know about things, and how competent we are to evaluate even what little we know or think we know. This is very plainly the case in foreign affairs. But the average person to whom this book is addressed is not an expert in diplomacy; he needs only to contribute his opinions to the democratic control of foreign policy (if it can be done anymore).

But in his more immediate situation he must make his own decisions, and should. If it is true that one's opinions are no better than his facts, then situation ethics puts a high premium on our knowing what's what when we act. We are always free and often well advised to call in expert and professional advice *if we choose* to call upon it. But if law cuts down our range of free initiative and personal responsibility, by doing our thinking for us, we are so much the less for it as persons. Law easily undermines political freedom (democracy) and personal freedom (grace).

Situation ethics aims to widen freedom, which is the other face of responsibility. As much as he can, the situationist will prevent law's Procrusteanly squeezing down an iron system of prefabricated decisions upon free

[16] Paul Tillich, *Systematic Theology*, Vol. I (1951), p. 153.

people in living situations. He is data conscious because
the alternative is to be sub-Christian and subhuman. He
faces the information explosion of this scientific era un-
afraid. One recalls with joy the candor of a Church
Assembly Commission (Anglican) in 1962 which reported that the traditional legalistic prohibition of sterilization for nontherapeutic reasons should be acknowledged to
be "wrong," after all, because of new data!

If it is supposed that the situational method of moral
decision-making is too open to a conscious or unconscious
rationalizing of selfish and evasive motives, we need only
to remember that self-deceit and excuse-making can ex-
ploit *law* too for its own purposes, often as easily as it
uses freedom. Our real motives can hide as effectively
behind rules as behind free contextual choices. Law is a
common camouflage, and makes a much better disguise.
It is harder to hide double-dealing when you have no
protective cover of law. Being legally right may mean
nothing at all morally, as any acquaintance with money
lenders and technical virgins will show. H. G. Wells once
said that a lot of moral indignation is "only jealousy with
a halo."

No. The plain fact is that love is an imperious law unto
itself. It will not share its power. It will not share its
authority with any other laws, either natural or supernatural. Love is even capable of desecrating the Holy of
Holies, the very tabernacle of the altar, if human hunger
cries for help. Imagine an Anglo-Catholic or Roman
Catholic being told that in serious need of food it is all
right to open the pyx and eat the Blessed Sacrament!
What a shock to law-bound piety! The pericope Matt.
12:1–8 (and parallels Mark 2:23–28; Luke 6:1–5)
left no doubt about Jesus' willingness to follow the radical
decisions of love. He puts his stamp of approval on the
translegality of David's paradigm or exemplary act: "Have
you never read what David did, when he was . . . hungry,

he and those who were with him: how he entered the
house of God . . . and ate the bread of the Presence,
which it is not lawful for any but the priests to eat, and
also gave it to those who were with him?" At least the
Christ of the Christian ethic leaves no doubt whatsoever
that *the ruling norm of Christian decision is love: nothing
else.*

V

Love and Justice Are the Same

The Third Proposition: "Love and justice are the same, for justice is love distributed, nothing else."

HERE IS A PROPOSITION that illuminates many of casuistry's shadows. Indeed, it throws light into dark corners at many levels of Christian ethics. Practically every problem of perplexed conscience, as distinguished from a doubtful conscience, can be reduced to the tension between love and justice. Let's not forget that Augustine, for all his insistence on the centrality of love, was compelled to explain that love's administration needs "more than good will, and can be done only by a high degree of thoughtfulness and prudence."[1]

LOVE IS CAREFUL

This is why he used the *dilectio* (*diligere*)—not *amor* or *caritas*—to emphasize the love that not only cares but is *careful*, "diligent" in serving the neighbor as well as it can. Prudence and love are not just partners, they are one and the same. That is to say, *Christian* love and *Christian*

[1] "Morals of the Catholic Church," 26:25, in Philip Schaff, ed., *Nicene and Ante-Nicene Fathers* (Buffalo: Christian Literature Co., 1887), Vol. IV, p. 55.

prudence are one and the same, since they both go out to
others. (Self-centered love and prudence are something
else altogether!)

This is a side of love that businessmen can appreciate,
as when a production engineer tries to balance product
quality against price in a low-income market; or a per-
sonnel manager has to choose between letting an illness-
weakened supply clerk keep his job, on the one hand, and
on the other, playing fair with line workers whose output
and piece-rate pay are being cut down by the clerk's delays.
Love as prudence helps a field commander who has to
decide whether a platoon or company, or even a regiment,
is expendable. And if so, which one. Prudence, careful
calculation, gives love the care-fulness it needs; with
proper care, love does more than take justice into account,
it *becomes* justice.

When we see love in this way we are forced to pull
back from the sentimental and irrational idea that love
isn't "intellectual." Luther was speaking of faith when he
said, "Whoever wants to be a Christian should gouge out
the eyes of reason"[2] because reason is "the devil's bride,
. . . a lovely whore."[3] Too many Christians think this
nonrationality applies to love too. It does not.

Here is precisely the serious difficulty of love. How are
its favors to be distributed among so many beneficiaries?
We never have one neighbor at a time. How are we to
love justice, how are we to be just about love, how are
love and justice related? If to love is to seek the neighbor's
welfare, and justice is being fair as between neighbors,
then how do we put these two things together in our *acts,*
in the situation? The answer is that in the Christian ethic
the twain become one. Even if we define justice as giving

[2] *What Luther Says, An Anthology,* compiled by E. M.
Plass (Concordia Publishing House, 1959), Vol. I, p. 90.

[3] *Luther's Works,* Vol. 51, ed. and tr. by John W. Dober-
stein (Muhlenberg Press, 1959), p. 374.

to others what is their due, we must redefine it Christianly. For what *is* it that is due to our neighbors? It is love that is due—*only* love ("Owe no man anything except to love"). Love is justice, justice is love.

Again granting that justice is giving to each man what is his due (the *suum cuique* of Aristotle and Thomas Aquinas), how are we to calculate, weigh, and distribute love's benefits among so many? As "persons" we are individuals-in-community. Therefore love's outreach is many-sided and wide-aimed, not one-directional; it is pluralist, not monist; multilateral, not unilateral. Agapeic love is not a one-to-one affair. (That would be *philia* or *erōs*.) Love uses a shotgun, not a rifle! Faced as we always are in the social complex with a web of duties, i.e., giving what is "due" to others, love is compelled to be calculating, careful, prudent, distributive. It must be omnified, taking everything into account, and optimific, doing all that it can.

Wrongful Separation

It will not do merely to keep love and justice separate, and then to give one or the other priority. Nathaniel Micklem relates a story of Canon Quick's about an Indian deeply in debt who inherited a fortune and gave it away to the poor, leaving his creditors unpaid.[4] The "moral" drawn was that something is wrong with charity (love) when it is at variance with justice, since charity does more than justice, not less. This is, of course, a very badly drawn lesson. It is true, yes, that love and justice should not be at variance. The reason, however, is not that one should excel the other but, rather, that they are one and the same thing and *cannot* vary! The Indian failed in *agapē*, and was therefore unjust.

Justice is the many-sidedness of love. Love's simplest

[4] *Law and the Laws* (Edinburgh: William Green & Son, Ltd., 1952), p. 115.

complication is "commutative" justice or one-to-one obligation, as in buying and selling or making contracts, *ex-
changing* goods or values. It becomes more complex with
"distributive" justice or many-to-one, when, e.g., the community shares out its assets with citizens in retirement
benefits or frames a fair law for selective service. In the
reverse direction and equally complex is "contributive"
justice or one-to-many, as when a man pays his taxes
or a club committee figures out a reasonable dues charge.
The institutional problem of social ethics, "corporative"
justice or many-to-many, wrestles with love's problems in
union-management relations, international affairs, trade
treaties, United Nations policy, and the like. To say that
love is between individuals and justice between groups,
and that a union cannot "love" a corporation or a city
cannot love the nation, is to sentimentalize love and
dehumanize justice.

After a thorough and brilliant exposition of the radical
intensity of an agapeic love ethic, Paul Ramsey was in
the end forced by his own logic to insist that love is, so
to speak, in honor bound to figure the angles.[5] Love's
calculations, which the Greeks called prudence, keep
love's imagination sharpened and at work. It saves love
from any sentimental myopia or selective blindness as it
does its work. Each of its claimants must be heard in
relation to the others. This is the operational and situational discipline of the love ethic—it needs to find *absolute love's relative course.* The what and the why are
given but the how and the which must be found.

> "I keep six honest serving men,
>   (They taught me all I knew);
>   Their names are What and Why and When
>   And How and Where and Who."

[5] *Basic Christian Ethics* (Charles Scribner's Sons, 1950),
p. 347.

In all humility and in spite of any hesitations based on false piety and Biblicism, Christian ethics is under grave obligation to do some tinkering with Scripture—i.e., with translations from the Greek of the Summary. And why? Because we have to add an "s" to "neighbor" in that distillation of the law. In order to make sure that *agapē* is not sentimentalized and individualized, reduced to a merely one-to-one relationship (this is the essence of pietistic distortion), we must render the generic term *plēsion* in the plural form "neighbors." The plural is there implicitly but practical conscience and good hermeneutics have to make it explicit. Only thus can we avoid the over-simplifying Tolstoyan notion that love wears blinders, never calculates, sees only the one-to-one *immediate* neighbor, the one who simply happens to be *nigh* or right there under your nose. We must sophisticate the childish notion that love is only for people one at a time.

Even "social gospel" moralists have been pietistic about love. Rauschenbusch, speaking of a man's concern for his neighbor, said, "If he loves him, let him love him enough to be just to him."[6] How can you love him if you are not just to him? Even if we accept the separation of the two, which we don't, surely "love" would *start* by being just—as the very least it could do.

A few years ago Sammy Davis, Jr., a popular American entertainer, repudiated his Christian identity and became a Jew. "As I see it," he said, "the difference is that the Christian religion preaches love thy neighbor and the Jewish religion preaches justice, and I think justice is the big thing we need."[7] Here is the cry of a man who has suffered discrimination, and seen millions of other Negroes suffer, because people separate love and justice.

[6] Walter Rauschenbusch, *Christianizing the Social Order* (The Macmillan Company, 1912), p. 332.
[7] *Esquire Magazine,* October, 1959.

On this basis they can "love" Negroes while they refuse them simple justice! To paraphrase the classic cry of protest, we can say, "To hell with your 'love'; we want justice." To understand such a battle cry is to see how pietism and sentimentality have twisted and shortchanged *agapē*.

What untold foolishness and moral purblindness have been caused by the individualizing error of pietism! Tolstoy was one of its staunchest exponents. In the first place, he tried to hold that love is a one-to-one affair, that it wears blinders like a shy horse and has only one neighbor at a time. (The fear that calculation may thin down love's intensity is a "calculated risk" built into its open-range, wide-scope task.) In the second place, he made love a matter of immediate, present neighbor concern with no thought of the morrow, no calculation of future needs. He literalized the Sermon's admonition: "Take therefore no thought for the morrow. . . . Sufficient unto the day is the evil thereof!" "Future love does not exist," he said. "Love is a present activity only."[8] A love that casts aside breadth of vision and imaginative foresight in this fashion is ethically crippled. Sad to say, it is not at all rare: the name for it is sentimentality.

A Proposed Reunion

However, the main thing to emphasize is that only a misdirected conscience has to wrestle with the "justice *versus* love" problem. It is seen to be a pseudoproblem at once when we drop the traditional *systematic* habit of separating them as "virtues." There is an interesting parallel between the love-justice and faith-works syndromes. Some theologies treat faith-works as faith *versus* works, some as faith *or* works, some as faith *and* works.

[8] Leo Tolstoy, *On Life,* tr. by Aylmer Maude (Oxford University Press, 1934), p. 98.

Christian situation ethics says faith *is* works, i.e., simply put, that faith works. In the same way various systems of Christian ethics have related love and justice: love *versus* justice (opposites),[9] love *or* justice (alternatives),[10] love *and* justice (complements).[11] We say, however, very positively, that love *is* justice or that justice loves. They are one and the same. To be loving is to be just, to be just is to be loving.

The tendency to reify, to imagine that predicates are actually properties, is as potent in the case of justice as of love. Psychologically, it becomes easier to separate them into different entities when they are supposed to *be* something. Nygren with his motif research separated and opposed them, putting justice in *erōs* or self-interest and love in *agapē* or disinterestedness.[12] So did Denis de Rougemont.[13] Reinhold Niebuhr separated and made them alternatives, love transcendent and impossible, justice relative and possible.[14] (Rather than saying with Niebuhr that love is ideal and justice is actual, we should be saying that love is maximum justice and justice is optimum love.) Emil Brunner and William Temple have separated them, assigning love to interpersonal relations and justice to intergroup relations. All Catholic moralists separate them, making love a "supernatural" virtue and justice a "natural"

[9] See Anders Nygren's *Agape and Eros*, tr. by Philip S. Watson (The Westminster Press, 1953).

[10] Reinhold Niebuhr, *The Nature and Destiny of Man* (Charles Scribner's Sons, 1941–1943), Vol. II, pp. 245 ff.

[11] William Temple, *Christianity and Social Order* (London: SCM Press, Ltd., 1950), p. 75; Emil Brunner, *Justice and the Social Order* (London: Lutterworth Press, 1945), pp. 114–118, 125. Also, see any competent work in Roman Catholic moral theology.

[12] *Agape and Eros*.

[13] *Love in the Western World* (Pantheon Books, 1956).

[14] His constructive ethics is equivocal because he uses "mutual love," meaning a relative "possible" love.

one, holding that we *must* be just in our actions but only
may be loving! (The very absurdity of this for a Christian
ethic shows that something is seriously wrong here at the
outset, for Catholic theologians are the very model of
logical system builders.)

Tillich links them in a coalition, a mutual reinforce-
ment. He says that love "is the ground, the power, and
the aim of justice," so that "love without justice is a body
without a backbone."[15] He comes fairly close to coalescing
them, to making them the same thing. He agrees that love
is "the ultimate principle of justice."[16] But this is not
close enough. He does not say, as we must say, that justice
is the "ultimate" principle of love. In like fashion, G.
Ernest Wright and Canon Quick say that justice is an
aspect of love, inseparable from it, but they are really
including one in the other—they are not equating them.[17]
Ramsey once said that "justice may be defined as what
Christian love does when confronted by two or more
neighbors."[18] The trouble with this is that love *always*
confronts many neighbors.

The "love, not justice" and "justice, not love" gambits
have completely muddied the waters of all ethics, Christian and non-Christian. Ethical relativism, as in situation
ethics, has to bury it once and for all. As we shall see in
the next chapter, a lot of our trouble can be traced to an
inveterate tendency to make love a sentiment rather than
a formal principle, to romanticize it or assign it to friendship, as Brunner and Temple do (interpersonal as divided

[15] *The Theology of Culture* (Oxford University Press,
1959), pp. 133–145.
[16] *Love, Power and Justice* (Oxford University Press,
1954), p. 79.
[17] Wright, *The Biblical Doctrine of Man in Society* (London: SCM Press, Ltd., 1954), p. 168; O. C. Quick, *Christianity and Justice* (London: Sheldon Press, 1940), p. 25.
[18] *Basic Christian Ethics*, p. 243.

from intergroup). But Christianly speaking, we know that this is wrong; that *agapē* is what is due to all others, to our various and many neighbors whether we "know" them or not. Justice is nothing other than love working out its problems. This viewpoint has existed potentially for a long time. Now we state it flatly and starkly so that there is no mistaking what is said. Love=justice; justice=love.

It is often said that what is "due" to the neighbor is giving him his "rights." But here again we see that for situation ethics the same reasoning obtains. You have a right to anything that is loving; you have no right to anything that is unloving. All alleged rights and duties are as contingent and relative as all values. The right to religious freedom, free speech, public assembly, private property, sexual liberty, life itself, the vote—*all* are validated only by love.

LOVE USING ITS HEAD

Justice is Christian love using its head, calculating its duties, obligations, opportunities, resources. Sometimes it is hard to decide, but the dilemmas, trilemmas, and multilemmas of conscience are as baffling for legalists as for situationists.[19] Justice is love coping with situations where distribution is called for. On this basis it becomes plain that as the love ethic searches seriously for a social policy it must form a coalition with utilitarianism. It takes over from Bentham and Mill the strategic principle of "the greatest good of the greatest number."

Observe that this is a genuine coalition, even though it reshapes the "good" of the utilitarians, replacing their pleasure principle with *agapē*. In the coalition the hedonistic calculus becomes the agapeic calculus, the greatest amount of neighbor welfare for the largest number of neighbors possible. It uses the procedural principle of

[19] Leonard Hatch, *Dilemmas* (Simon and Schuster, Inc., 1931).

utilitarianism, distribution of benefits, but it already has
its value principle as given in the Summary.

We need not try to assert some supposed mutual exclusion as between *agapē* and the "happiness" that utilitarians
want. All depends upon what we find our happiness in:
all ethics are happiness ethics. With hedonists it is one's
own pleasure (physical or mental); with neo-Aristotelians
it is self-realization; with naturalists it is adjustment,
gratification, and survival. Happiness is the pragmatist's
satisfaction.[20] It is "how you get your kicks." The Christian
situationist's happiness is in doing God's will as it is
expressed in Jesus' Summary. And his utility method sets
him to seeking his happiness (pleasure, too, and self-
realization!) by seeking his neighbors' good on the widest
possible scale.

(Words such as "happiness" and "pleasure" are not
definitive. Attempts to systematize ethics always break
down at this level. Hedonism, naturalism, utilitarianism—
these are really hardly more than epithets. The same holds
true of class terms such as "deontological" for formal or
duty ethics, said to be concerned with doing the right
rather than seeking the good; and "teleological" for *goal*
or aspiration ethics, said to be concerned with realizing
the good more and more, not merely obeying a law or
rules.[21] In these conventional terms situation ethics is
closer to teleology, no doubt. Yet one's "duty" is to seek
the goal of the most love possible in every situation, and
one's "goal" is to *obey* the command to do just that! Our
goal is to obey the Summary; our obedience is to serve
love's aim and aspiration. Here is double-talk; there is no

[20] Each Beatitude begins, *"Happy* are . . ."* the poor, the
meek, the merciful, etc. (Gr. *makarioi*).

[21] Edward Duff, S. J., does this with "an ethic of ends"
(Catholic) and "an ethic of inspiration" or obedience to the
love commandment (Protestant), in *Social Teaching of the
World Council of Churches* (Association Press, 1956), p. 93.

difference *in practice*. Calm scrutiny breaks down many of these neat and artificial categories.)

Take the story of the anointing at Bethany.[22] (John's Gospel uses the episode to attack Judas, but Mark and Matthew let the real issue appear.) The issue is between impetuous, uncalculating, unenlightened sentimental love, in the woman's use of the costly ointment, and a calculating, enlightened love. The disciples say that love must work in coalition with utilitarian distribution, spreading the benefits as much as possible. Jesus is cast into the role of defending Leo Tolstoy's doctrine that love wears blinders, sees only the neighbor *there*. If we take the story as it stands, Jesus was wrong and the disciples were right. Attempts have been made to excuse Jesus, saying he was trying to comfort the thoughtless but sincere woman, softening the criticism of the bystanders while he actually agreed with them. We do not have to conclude that he ever said anything at all like, "You always have the poor with you."

When Ivar Kreuger's suicide showed that investments in his operations were worthless, in 1932, one American brokerage firm used its privy knowledge of the fact to sell its shares and those of its clients on the exchange to the ignorant trading public. This showed a proper concern for its own and its clients' welfare, but it was a clear betrayal of agapeic (all-loving) care. Love does not permit us to solve our problems or soothe our wounds at the expense of innocent third parties. Our neighbors include *all* our neighbors.

A resident physician on emergency, deciding whether to give the hospital's last unit of blood plasma to a young mother of three or to an old skid row drunk, may suppose that he is being forced to make a tragic choice between "disinterested" love and justice. He may have been sentimentalized into thinking that to choose the mother and

[22] Mark 14:3–9; Matt. 26:6–13; John 12:1–8.

her children means ignoring love's "impartial" concern for all neighbors alike. But this falsifies reality. There is no partiality, no "respecting of persons," in preferring to serve more rather than fewer, many rather than few. Love *must* make estimates; it *is* preferential. That is to say, it is responsible, thoughtful, careful. To prefer the mother *in that situation* is the most loving decision. And therefore it is the most just decision too.

When T. E. Lawrence led his Arab forces against the Turks, he had to make moral choices, being a responsible decision maker. Hamed the Moor killed Salem in a personal quarrel while they were camped in the Wadi Kitan, even though Lawrence tried to stop it. He knew that Salem's people would exact "justice" by revenge, starting an endless feud and bloodletting. How should he calculate? He himself killed Hamed, to end it. Here is a real problem love faced. Bonhoeffer made the same *kind* of choice when he became a partner in the plot to kill Hitler. On a vast scale of "agapeic calculus" President Truman made his decision about the A-bombs on Hiroshima and Nagasaki.

Since legalistic casuistry says we are not always bound to be "loving," it *might* comfort Dr. Arrowsmith in Sinclair Lewis' novel. The scientist decided to give his new serum to only half the people on an island of the Caribbean, letting the others die of a plague, in order to convince skeptical authorities and so save many more lives in other epidemics. But legalistic casuistry could not comfort the British intelligence staff in World War II, when they let a number of women agents return to Germany to certain arrest and death in order to keep secret the fact that they had broken the German code. Situational casuistry could easily approve their decision.

If love does not calculate both the immediate and the remote consequence of its decisions, it turns selfish, childish, soft, subverting its own limitless, all-embracing work. To imagine that conscience may sometimes deny love but never justice, as the "natural law" theologians do, is confusion worse confounded. Such a demotion of love is perhaps the best they can do, given their initial mistake of separating love and justice as "virtues"—as properties to be "infused" rather than predicates of action. Actually, our only choice is between sentimentality and discernment, not between love and justice. *Love and justice are the same, for justice is love distributed, nothing else.*

ADDENDUM

We have been speaking of justice as a moral principle, not as something settled and static, transfixed in laws. The root *jus* means many things: law, both written and unwritten; rights; and standards or ideals. But the basic distinction to be grasped is between *moral* justice and legal justice. The two, of course, are not antithetical, but it must be fully recognized that legal justice (law) always threatens to suffocate and cheat moral justice. Statutory laws, both civil and criminal, and the common law or custom, as in the Anglo-American tradition and most cultures, are in the situationist's view a necessary danger —but not, note, *necessarily* evil.

It is the task of jurisprudence, the philosophy and ethics of law and legislation, to keep legal justice as close as possible to moral justice. Most judicial systems even include, as a court of last resort, a procedure called equity in which it is sometimes admitted that although "the law was broken," the wrongdoer *in the situation* could not have acted otherwise without betraying moral justice too grossly to let even legalists close their eyes to it. This task of equity and jurisprudence is all bound up in, when it is not tied down by, the conflicting attitudes and tempers of jurists who are agapeic about justice and those who are legalists. The latter say with unction and every appearance of righteousness, "Rules are rules, laws are laws; don't blame me, you can't satisfy everybody."

To some, justice means merely *penal* justice, "giving them what they deserve" according to an established code of rewards and punishments. To some, it means an impartial, evenhanded administration of law, and to others, a fair adjudication between rival claims. Aristotle long ago distinguished between arithmetical justice, under which laws assume an identity between persons and cases, judging them according to the book, and geometrical justice, under which laws assume variety between persons and situations, judging cases more on their own merits and aiming at proportion between real people—although within the abstractions of "public order."

The old cracker-barrel phrase is: "We can't legislate morals." Experience with sex laws, as with the "noble experiment" of prohibition in the twenties, seems to support that idea. But sometimes law can encourage and inculcate higher standards of behavior, not reflecting present mores but nurturing and pioneering better ones. Situationists acknowledge that law and order are not only necessary but actually good, wherever and whenever they promote the best interests of love.

Christian ethics is concerned not only with a remedy for sin (moral evil), as in discrimination against Negroes, but also with the *restraint* of it. It needs both love-justice and law-order. Indeed, each presupposes the other. Situation ethics welcomes law for love's sake sometimes, all depending. This is why anarchism is a fallacious social idealism, and why Tolstoy was wrong. It recognizes the need for love but fails to see the need for order. It sees the importance of voluntary order but is too myopic toward the reality of sin to see the need for *a loving use of force* to protect the innocent and to make "rights" practicable.

But desegregation laws and adequate civil rights legislation are essential to justice understood agapeically. Whenever or if ever any civil rights law ceases to serve love according to an enlightened grasp of love's outreach, it should be thrown aside. We have a moral obligation to obey civil law, for order's sake; and we have a moral obligation to be situational (even disobeying the law) for love's sake. This statement is beamed to both segregationists and integrationists. Law and freedom from law can be duties, but love is the basic principle.

In this connection we should note that the strategy of civil disobedience poses the problem neatly. We ought not to hesitate to break a law that is in all conscience unjust, that is to say, unloving. Perhaps also we should before or *pari passu* do what we can to get it reinterpreted in the courts or thrown out on some ground such as constitutionality, using legislative machinery to correct it. But neither the state nor its laws is boss for the situationist; when there is a conflict, he decides for the higher law of love.[23] He has to weigh immediate and remote consequences as well as local and broader interests, but if the scales go against law, so does he.

If his disobedience is ethical, not sheer outlawry, he will be open and aboveboard about it. His disobedience will be a witness to love-justice, and doing it in plain view will be his acknowledgment of order's reasonable claims.[24] The serious subversive is never clandestine. Yet we should note that there is always the more radical possibility that the conscientious revolt is not against any particular law so much as against the state itself, presumably on the ground that omnific and optimific love has decided finally that the state behind the law is beyond love's pale. Love then requires revolution. In this case, obviously, conspiracy rather than open witness is the right way.

In the American Revolution, the Boston "tea party,"

[23] One Christian moralist condemns this view, R. C. Mortimer, *Christian Ethics* (London: Hutchinson's Universal Library, 1950), pp. 57 ff.

[24] See J. A. Pike's thoughtful discussion, *op. cit.*, pp. 98–102, 106–108.

which threw casks of tea into the harbor in protest against unjust revenues, was an instance of civil disobedience, whereas the patriots' subsequent secret raising of citizen armies to fight the Redcoats was revolution. The one can escalate into the other, but need not and ought not so to escalate until serious analysis combines with loyalty to freedom to make it a demand of enlightened love-justice.

But the basic point is that moral justice is not legal justice. In Melville's symbolic tragedy *Billy Budd,* Claggart's lies accusing Billy of taking part in the mutiny plans drove the tongue-tied and shocked Billy into hitting him. The blow accidentally killed him. Everybody knew that Billy was innocent, and of the stress he was under. The ship's officers would have found him innocent in a court-martial. But Captain Vere convinced them that their duty was to apply the articles of war, with their law that a sailor who strikes a superior officer (here a foretopman hitting a master-at-arms) is to be hanged. Vere was afraid of the mutinous British crew, many of whom, like Billy, had been forcibly impressed. So they hanged Billy. Vere was loyal to the law, not to love. But in scorning love he scorned justice too. Only law won.[25]

This story vividly portrays how law, not freedom, can be used to rationalize and disguise selfish motives and personal prejudices. To say that situation ethics could do any worse is either naïve or perverse. It happens all the time.

[25] *Shorter Novels of Herman Melville* (Liveright Publishing Corporation, 1928).

VI

Love Is Not Liking

*The Fourth Proposition: "Love wills the neigh-
bor's good whether we like him or not."*

To LOVE CHRISTIANLY is a matter of attitude, not of feeling. Love is discerning and critical; it is not sentimental.
Many students of Christian ethics have quarreled with
one thing or another in Anders Nygren's *Agape and Eros*
since its appearance in 1932, coincidentally with Brunner's basic ethical work and Niebuhr's. But as to its core
thesis, that Christian love is definitely agapeic, not erotic
nor philic (not a question of romance or friendship),
there has been no serious debate. That is, it is neighbor-
concerned, outgoing, not self-concerned or selective.

(Even when Plato in the *Symposium* or the *Phaedrus*
used *erōs* with a spiritualized meaning, it was still primarily in the lover's own interest and for his own sake.
And when Father Martin D'Arcy protests, rightly, that
the two loves, *agapē* and *erōs,* are not mutually exclusive,
he is not actually questioning the distinction or its importance.[1])

NEVER SENTIMENTALIZE LOVE

In Canon Quick's sensitive expression, "Whereas in
erōs desire is the cause of love, in *agapē* love is the cause

[1] *The Mind and Heart of Love* (Henry Holt & Company,
Inc., 1947), pp. 54 ff.

of desire."[2] *Agapē's* desire is to satisfy the neighbor's need,
not one's own, but the main thing about it is that *agapē*
love precedes all desire, of any kind. It is not at all an
emotional norm or motive. It is volitional, conative. The
ethic of *agapē* is a *Gesinnungs-ethik,* an attitudinal ethic.
This is why Rudolf Bultmann is so positive in his statement: "In reality, the love which is based on emotions of
sympathy, or affection, is self-love; for it is a love of
preference, of choice, and the standard of the preference
and choice is the self."[3]

A young unmarried couple might decide, if they make
their decisions Christianly, to have intercourse (e.g., by
getting pregnant to force a selfish parent to relent his over-
bearing resistance to their marriage). But as Christians
they would never merely say, "It's all right if we *like* each
other!" Loving concern can make it all right, but mere
liking cannot.

Richardson's *Theological Word Book* explains that the
predominant New Testament verb for love, *agapaō,* "has
neither the warmth of *phileō* nor the intensity of *eraō,*"
and refers to "the will rather than to emotion."[4] Bishop
Stephen Neill calls it "the steady directing of the human
will towards the eternal well-being of another."[5] According
to Søren Kierkegaard, to say that love is a feeling or anything of that kind is an unchristian conception of love.[6]
H. R. Niebuhr and Waldo Beach have asserted flatly that

[2] *The Doctrines of the Creed* (Charles Scribner's Sons,
1938), p. 54.

[3] *Jesus and the Word,* p. 117.

[4] C. E. B. Cranfield, "Love," in Alan Richardson, ed.,
Theological Word Book of the Bible (London: SCM Press,
Ltd., 1951), pp. 131–136.

[5] Quoted in F. D. Coggan, *The New Testament Basis of
Moral Theology* (London: Tyndale Press, 1948), p. 8.

[6] *The Journals,* tr. by Alexander Dru (Oxford University
Press, 1938), entry 932, p. 317.

"Christ's love was not an inner feeling, a full heart and what not; it was the *work* of love, which was his life."[7] C. H. Dodd said of *agapē* that "it is not primarily an emotion or affection; it is primarily an active determination of the will. That is why it can be commanded, as feelings cannot."[8] Those for whom true love is an emotion will naturally take hate to be its opposite; those who follow the Biblical understanding will readily see that its opposite is indifference, simply not caring.

(We appreciate the pitfalls of oversimplified word studies. We cannot really construct a conceptual apparatus or Biblical theology on words alone; it requires whole statements.[9] Yet on any approach to the problem, linguistic or not, the same nonemotional understanding of the key terms *agapē* in the New Testament, and *aheb* and *hesed* in the Old, results.)

Pinned down to its precise meaning, Christian love is benevolence, literally. Goodwill. Unfortunately for us in our age, if we have any wish to stick with the New Testament's glossary of terms, the words "benevolence" and "goodwill" have by common usage taken on a tepid, almost merely polite meaning. Nevertheless, this is what Christian love is. It does not seek the deserving, nor is it judgmental when it makes its decisions—judgmental, that is, about the people it wants to serve. *Agapē* goes out to our neighbors not for our own sakes nor for theirs, really, but for God's. We can say quite plainly and colloquially that Christian love is the business of loving the unlovable, i.e., the *unlikable*.

This love is as radical as it is because of its non-reciprocal, noncongenial outreach. It is for the deserving

[7] *Christian Ethics* (The Ronald Press Co., 1955), p. 438.

[8] *Gospel and Law* (Columbia University Press, 1951), p. 42.

[9] See, e.g., James Barr, *The Semantics of Biblical Language* (Oxford University Press, 1961), pp. 263 ff.

and the undeserving alike. God makes his sun rise on the evil and on the good, and sends rain on the just and the unjust. To suppose that we are required by any Christian imperative to like everybody is a cheap hypocrisy ethically and an impossibility psychologically. People often point out, quite reasonably and properly, that "it is impossible to love in obedience to a command" and that to ask it of us only encourages hypocrisy, "since all men are not lovable."[10] Both objections are correct. But only if we *sentimentalize* love, taking it to be a matter of feeling or emotion, could they be true objections to *agapē*. Loving and liking are not the same thing.

Kant observed that love cannot be commanded, and discussed the question at some length.[11] In his own way and in his own language he recognized that romantic love (and, for that matter, friendship love) cannot be ordered at all. But *agapē* can. He concluded that in Jesus' Summary, in the second part, "it is only *practical* love that is meant in that pith of all laws." There is nothing sentimental about Christian love or Christian ethics.

Admittedly, there can be no command, no obligation, no duty, to love if love is affection, as it most assuredly is in friendship love (*philia*). Genuine emotion—what psychologists call "affect" to mark it off from conation or will—cannot be turned on and off like water from a faucet, simply by an act of will or willing obedience to a command. But the works of will, of love, *can!*

Kindness, generosity, mercy, patience, concern, righteous indignation, high resolve—these things are "virtues" or dispositions of the will, attitudes or leanings, and therefore they are, psychologically speaking, perfectly possible requirements of covenant and command. (A typical list-

[10] Cf. E. B. Redlich, *The Forgiveness of Sins* (Edinburgh: T. & T. Clark, 1937), pp. 294–295.

[11] *Critique of Practical Reason,* tr. by T. K. Abbott (Longmans, Green & Co., Inc., 1923), p. 176.

ing by Paul of virtues, of fruits of the Spirit, as in Gal.
5:22, amply manifests their conative rather than affective
character.)

THE NEIGHBOR IS ANYBODY

With the bluntest extremism Matt. 5:43–48 sharpens
agapē's radical thrust: "Love your enemies. . . . For if
you love those who love you, what reward have you?"
What more, that is to say, do you accomplish with philic
love than anybody else? Friendship, romance, self-realization—all these loves are reciprocal. *Agapē* is not. It seeks
the good of anybody, everybody.

The Greeks thought of love as need, demanding and
desiring. Socrates' story in the *Symposium* is typical: Eros
was born out of Penia (poverty). Among the Greeks, God
could not easily be called love, since to them God was
perfect, needing nothing. In the Biblical-Jewish view, love
is a phenomenon of strength. It goes out instead of taking
in. They had no trouble believing in a God who wants
and offers covenants; who would mount a cross for man's
sake. He is love and he gives himself and he is inexhaustible; love is inexhaustible.

The radical obligation of the Christian ethic is to love
not only the stranger-neighbor and the acquaintance-
neighbor but even the enemy-neighbor, just as we love
the friend-neighbor. Every neighbor is not friendly nor a
friend. To suppose they are is to be sentimental and uncritical, i.e., antiagapeic. Christian love does not ask us
to lose or abandon our sense of good and evil, or even of
superior and inferior; it simply insists that however we
rate them, and whether we like them or not, they are our
neighbors and are to be loved.

There are some neighbors who, being what they are
now, simply could not be one's friend. Most of us—all
except the hypocrites and the hopeless sentimentalizers—
know any number of people whom we seriously do not like,

often for sufficient cause, often for no particular reason. (*Agapē* demands, however, that when *philia* is lacking, we must lean over backward to love those we don't like! "One cannot command that one *feel* love for a person but only that one deal lovingly with him."[12])

But Christian love, which is not at all reciprocal, not *mutual*, is not concerned so much for a "close relationship" as for a dialogic encounter (to use Buber's phrase). It · does not presuppose any return of concern, even though it hopes for it. It is, in short, not a bargaining principle or a market orientation, as Erich Fromm would say.[13] It is, to recall what was said in the preceding chapter, an ethic in which justice—impartial, inclusive justice—and love are one and the same thing. As we know, justice is as personal as love, and love is as social as justice.

When the editor-compiler of Matthew's Sermon on the Mount ended his section on the universality and all-inclusiveness of love by saying "be perfect as your heavenly Father is," he could not have meant perfect in any maximal sense, of completeness. That is impossible for men. Given the section it summarizes, it can only mean one thing: be all-inclusive in your *agapē* as God is in his. And when *agapē* is understood to be will, the otherwise absurd commandment becomes of practicable seriousness.

This nonaffectional love is the Christian requirement as between man and God just as it is between man and man. Some, especially mystics and highly religious people, have a feeling (sometimes almost erotically intense) for God, for his very presence. Yet the nonreligious man who "knows" God only by faith commitment and willing obedience to his love command is as agapeic toward God as

[12] Martin Buber, *Two Types of Faith* (The Macmillan Company, 1952), p. 69.

[13] *Man for Himself: An Inquiry Into the Psychology of Ethics* (Rinehart & Co., Inc., 1947), pp. 67 ff.

those who have religious experience. One Anglican writer says of love, "It is a matter of choice, choosing to submit to the will of God."[14] Another says that "man is enabled to love God in the sense that by an act of will he prefers God above everything else."[15] Decision, will, is the key in both the man-to-God and man-to-man dimensions. Human relations can, of course, be both agapeic and philic. All that *agapē* stipulates is that we shall will another's good. Yet it is not without its significance that Christians find it much easier to have friendship for others when they start, at least, with love. Given the will, *philia* finds a way, discovers a reason to follow love. But when and if this happens, the feeling side is secondary—one of love's dividends.

Where were there ever more unlovable men than those who stood around the cross of Jesus, yet he said, "Forgive them"? Paul gave this its cosmic statement: "While we were yet sinners Christ died for us" (Rom. 5:8). Nonreciprocity and nondesert apply even to affection-love: Reuel Howe explains why "my child, your child, needs love most when he is most unlovable."[16] Good medical care prescribes "t.l.c." (tender loving care) every hour on the hour, whether doctors and nurses *like* the patient or not.

An egoistic ethic (erotic) says in effect, "My first and last consideration is myself." This is the essence of an exploitive stance; it is "what makes Sammy run." A mutualistic ethic (philic) says, "I will give as long as I receive." We all know this one because it is the common

[14] Herbert Waddams, *A New Introduction to Moral Theology* (London: SCM Press, Ltd., 1965), p. 122. See also his *Life and Fire of Love* (London: S.P.C.K., 1964).

[15] R. C. Mortimer, *The Elements of Moral Theology* (London: Longmans, Green & Co., Ltd., 1920), p. 43n.

[16] *Man's Need and God's Action* (The Seabury Press, Inc., 1953), p. 87.

dynamic of friendships. But an altruistic ethic (agapeic) says, "I will give, requiring nothing in return." It explains a Father Damien on Molokai, a kamikaze pilot, a patriot hiding in a Boston attic in 1775, or a Viet Cong terrorist walking into a Saigon officers' mess as he pulls the pin in a bomb hidden under his coat. All these actions, whether correctly (perhaps fanatically) decided or not, are examples of selfless, calculating concern for others. These three ethical postures spell out what is meant by the old saying, "There are only, after all, three kinds of ethics."

Self-love for the Neighbor's Sake

Just as neighbor-concern can find a place for friendship but need not, so it has a place for the self's good as well as the neighbor's, but always only if the self takes second place. *Agapē* is primarily other-regarding, yet secondarily it may be self-regarding. But if the self is ever considered, it will be for the neighbor's sake, not for the self's. "Love," says Paul (I Cor. 13:5), "does not insist on its own way."

But is self-love always selfish? Is it always opposed to *agapē*? Many think so, even though the second part of Jesus' Summary was, "You shall love your neighbor *as yourself*." Was this simple realism, recognizing that we *do* love ourselves (man's ego predicament), and commanding us to do for others what we are doing for ourselves? Or did it command us to do as *much* for others as for the self? Or did it actually constitute a command to love *ourselves* as well as to love God and neighbor?

This interesting formula seems to have had four main variant interpretations: (1) Love your neighbor just as much as you love yourself. (2) Love your neighbor in addition to loving yourself. (3) Love your neighbor in the way that you ought to love yourself. (4) Love your neighbor instead of loving yourself, as you have been doing heretofore but now must stop.

Each of the first three has some logical claim to acceptance, but the fourth is, to say the least, open to question. In the Thomistic view, Christian love is devotion to God and hence to his creatures, of whom each one of us is one; therefore we are to love ourselves as belonging to God. From another vantage point altogether, Kierkegaard also brought things together; he said, "To love one's self in the right way and to love one's neighbor are absolutely analogous concepts, are at bottom one and the same thing."[17] Therefore, he adds, "The commandment 'Love thy neighbor as thyself' means 'Thou shalt love thyself in the right way.' "[18]

This is psychologically shrewd. We cannot love others, nor can we be honest with them, if we are not able to love or be honest with ourselves. This is as true as it is to say that we cannot give love if we cannot accept it. Augustine asserted that "you love yourself suitably when you love God more than yourself."[19] In this formula we can substitute neighbor for God. Luther said that we "are Christs to one another," and, "The Christian man . . . lives in Christ through faith and in his neighbor through love."[20] In this love he gains himself.

Perhaps in some imaginative mystique it is possible to experience what Father Martin D'Arcy has called "ecstatic" love (a transport of love, heedless of self, off one's own center, utterly kenotic).[21] But self-realization, Christianly achieved by seeking the neighbor's good, seems to be a coinherence which outlaws any attempt by mutual exclusion to set the self over against the neighbor.

[17] *The Works of Love,* tr. by D. F. and L. M. Swenson (Princeton University Press, 1946), p. 17.

[18] *Ibid.,* p. 19.

[19] "Morals of the Catholic Church," 26:49, *loc cit.*

[20] "The Freedom of the Christian," in *Luther's Works,* Vol. 31, tr. by Harold J. Grimm (Concordia-Muhlenberg Press, 1957), pp. 367, 371.

[21] *The Mind and Heart of Love,* p. 29 *et seq.*

A long parade of eminent theologians and philosophers have insisted upon this: Plato, Aristotle, Augustine, Abelard, Luther, Aquinas, Butler, Jonathan Edwards. But the question remains, *how* are we to "love ourselves in the right way"? How are we to transform self-centered self-love into self-love for the sake of others? Agreeing that self-love is a given fact about people, are we to regard it, as some do, as wholly evil, preventing any good; or is it only a *danger*—on one of its sides the driving force behind creativity and fruitful struggle, on the other mere ego-centricity? In short, can the sin of self-regard be redeemed, can it be raised from selfishness to self-concern in the right way?

Bernard of Clairvaux, in a mystical and monkish essay, once outlined a "ladder" by which we may climb: It goes from (1) love of self for self's sake, to (2) love of God, yet still for self's sake, to (3) love of God for God's sake, to (4) love of self, once more, but this time for God's sake and not one's own.[22] In the same way, surely, we can see how it is possible, by a parallel, to ascend the ladder of neighbor-love: from (1) love of ourself for our own sake, to (2) love of our neighbor for our own sake, to (3) love of neighbor for the neighbor's sake, to (4) love of ourself again, but now *for the right reason,* i.e., for the neighbor's sake.

The meaning of this is, in a real way, that the Christian takes Aristotle's ideal of self-realization (self-nurture) seriously, but for the sake of his neighbors whom he will thereby be more fully able to serve, to whose welfare he may more solidly contribute. Better a trained man than a dolt, better for everybody.

But the problem of tragedy still haunts us, even if we (reader and author) are still together after the last flight

[22] *On the Love of God (De diligendo Deo)* newly tr. by a Religious of C.S.M.V. (Morehouse-Gorham, Inc., 1950), pp. 56–69.

of subtlety. The essence of tragedy is the conflict of one good or right with another. Tragedy, of necessity, brings creative casuistry into play. Melodrama, after all, is Sunday-school ethics, child's play—the conflict of good and evil. When we are asked to choose between the Good Guys and the Bad Guys, it is not too great a test of our ethical decision-making powers. But what of the situations in which the Lesser Evil and the Greater Good issue is posed? And to bring this to bear upon the problem of self-love, what do we do when self-love and neighbor-love cross each other?

Are the self's claims always to be denied in such cases? Surely not. The logic of love is that self-concern is obligated to cancel neighbor-good whenever *more* neighbor-good will be served through serving the self. The self is to be served rather than any neighbor if *many* neighbors are served through serving the self. This is strictly parallel to love's problem when facing a conflict between one neighbor's good and another's. We do not prefer one neighbor to another, but we *do* prefer the neighbor whose need is greater, and we prefer to serve *more* neighbors rather than fewer.

Therefore the ship's captain or the plane's pilot or the wagon train's or safari's master and scout—these are to keep themselves alive, even at the expense of some passengers, if need be, when disaster threatens all. This is tragedy—of the kind that is enacted constantly in peace and war. Who could seriously disagree with the situationist's opinion that the President of the United States, in the event of a bomb attack, should disregard all cries of fear, pain, and helplessness around him, and scuttle "callously" for the safety of his shelter, where his special knowledge could be brought to bear for millions of others?

The two commandments in the love Summary are really only one, and the three objects of love (God, neighbor, and self) unite its work; they do not divide it. All

love is *amor sui,* self-love, i.e., all love seeks its own good.
For Christians, self-love may be either right or wrong
love, depending upon the good sought and the situation.
If we love ourselves for our own sakes, that is wrong.
If we love ourselves for God's sake and the neighbor's, then
self-love is right. For to love God and the neighbor is to
love one's self in the right way; to love one's neighbor is
to respond to God's love in the right way; to love one's self
in the right way is to love God and one's neighbors.

CALCULATION IS NOT CRUEL

All of this is thoughtful love, careful as well as care-full.
It is a matter of intelligence, not sentiment. Nothing is as
complex and difficult as ethics, even Christian love ethics,
*once we have cut loose from law's oversimplifying pre-
tailored rules, once we become situational.* It was the
mature acceptance of this which lay behind Undershaft's
reply, when his son Stephen, the unemployed man-about-
town, said with considerable unction and self-righteous-
ness, and unbounded superficiality, "I know the difference
between right and wrong."

Said his father more annoyed than amused, "You don't
say so! What! no capacity for business, no knowledge of
law, no sympathy with art, no pretension to philosophy;
only a simple knowledge of the secret that has puzzled
all the philosophers, baffled all the lawyers, muddled all
the men of business, and ruined most of the artists: the
secret of right and wrong. Why man, you're a genius,
a master of masters, a god! At twenty-four, too!"[23] Stephen
is a prototype of ethical legalism.

Moral choices need intelligence as much as they need
concern, sound information as well as good disposition.

[23] Bernard Shaw, from *Major Barbara,* in *Selected Plays*
(Dodd, Mead & Company, Inc., 1948), Vol. I, p. 415. Used
by permission of The Public Trustee and The Society of
Authors.

To be "good" we have to get rid of innocence. The Victorian advice, "Be good, sweet maid, and let who will be clever," is false. The sweet maid *has* to bc clever to be good. We do not have to follow Socrates' identification of virtue and knowledge in order to insist upon the importance of facts, of context. The yogi alone is up in the air; he needs the commissar; aspiration needs practicality.

Even the radical principle of enemy-love has to be qualified in the calculations of the situation; it is right to deal lovingly with the enemy *unless to do so hurts too many friends.* The enemy-neighbor has no stronger claims than a friend-neighbor, after all. In the old heart tugger, "Which should you save if you can carry only one from a burning building, the baby or Da Vinci's *Mona Lisa?*" you take the baby if you are a personalist. There are copies and photos of the painting. But if the choice is between your own father and a medical genius who has discovered a cure for a common fatal disease, you carry out the genius if you understand *agapē.* This is the agapeic calculus. Sir David Ross tried to find a middle course between Kant's legalism and Mill's utility.[24] It was not a successful effort. Our situation ethics frankly joins forces with Mill; no rivalry here. We choose what is most "useful" for the most people.

In Italy during World War II a priest in the underground resistance bombed a Nazi freight train. The occupying authorities began killing twenty hostages a day, "until the saboteur surrendered." When asked if he refused to give himself up because he intended to do more heroic deeds, the priest said, "No. There is no other priest available and our people's souls need my absolution for their eternal salvation." After three days a Communist, a fellow resistance fighter, betrayed the priest to stop the carnage. One may accept the priest's assumptions about salvation or not (the Communist evidently did not), but

[24] See Ross, *The Right and the Good* (Oxford University Press, 1930).

no situationist could quarrel with his *method* of ethical analysis and decision.

Only those who sentimentalize and subjectivize love look upon calculation and "figuring the angles" as cold or cruel or inimical or a betrayal of "love's warmth." Tolstoy, who wanted love to be futureless (no consideration of consequences) and indifferent to arithmetic (no counting and weighing of one against another), seeing only the one who is *there,* was the soul of sentimentality. He would tell a doctor rushing to answer an emergency call for those hurt in an overturned bus to stop if, on the way, he saw a motorist smash into a wall. Quite to the contrary, love might even disguise itself, distort its face, pretend to be other than it is. In a TV play, *The Bitter Choice,* a nurse in a military hospital deliberately makes wounded soldiers hate her enough to motivate them to get them on their feet again and out of her care on the way to full recovery! Love can simulate, it can calculate. Otherwise, it is like the bride who wanted to ignore all recipes and simply let her love for her husband guide her when baking him a cake.

Some years ago a newsmagazine took up the perennial issue whether panhandlers should be turned away.[25] One minister wrote in that "of course they should be" sometimes, and in any case clergy ought not to give them money—never let the skillful panhandler outsmart them. Another minister wrote in to protest, calling his brother in the cloth "cold and suave" with "cold-as-ice efficiency," and arguing that clergy should meet immediate calls for help even if they are "taken" by the panhandler. But *agapē* is on the first man's side, assuming that he is not indifferent. This is why the Didache, that earliest of Christian ethical treatises, said, "Let thine alms sweat in thy palm until thou knowest to whom thou art to give." For love ethics, this is the bifocal vision of the serpent and the dove (Matt. 10:16).

[25] *Time,* November 26, 1956.

Make no mistake about it; love can not only make
people angry, it can *be* angry too. Love makes judgments;
it does not say, "Forget it" but, "Forgive it." It may not
hate the sinner but it hates the sin, to use an old but
fundamentally true bromide. This is why Augustine said,
right after his reduction of Christian ethics to a loving
will: "Love can be angry, charity can be angry, with a
kind of anger in which there is no gall, like the dove's and
not the raven's."[26]

Again, to love is not necessarily to please. *Agapē* is not
gratification. It has often been remarked that the golden
rule should read, "Do unto others as they would have you
do unto them"—that its classic form, "as you would have
them do unto you" is self-centered, cutting its cloth
according to what *you* want rather than what the neighbor
wants. But to accept this revision would be too close to
"disinterested" love; it would be *neutral* love, which is too
close to indifference. For *agapē* is concerned for the neighbor, ultimately, for God's sake; certainly not for the self's,
but not even for the neighbor's own sake only. Christian
love, for example, cannot give heroin to an addict just
because he wants it. Or, at least, if the heroin is given,
it will be given as part of a cure. And the same with
all pleas—sex, alms, food, anything. All parents know
this.

With the development of computers all sorts of analyt-
ical ethical possibilities open up. Legalism could find little
of interest in it but situation ethics does. Once we laughed
at Raimon Lull's medieval *Ars major,* an arithmetic, sure-
fire device for getting answers to theological questions.
It is said that followers of his in the "Lullian Science"
contrived a barrel device to revolve after fixing clock
pointers, so that a whirl of the barrel, like the spin of a

[26] "Seventh Homily on the First Epistle General of St.
John," in *Augustine: Later Works,* tr. by John Burnaby, The
Library of Christian Classics, Vol. VIII (The Westminster
Press, 1955), p. 318.

roulette wheel, would pop out the answer. In fact, it was a primitive computer.

It is possible that by learning how to assign numerical values to the factors at stake in problems of conscience, love's calculations can gain accuracy in an ethical *ars major*. The temper of situation ethics is in keeping with the attempt to quantify qualities. It is this kind of distributive analysis which modern game theory has matured.[27] And already game theory is being applied to ethics, as well as to economics, in our consideration of defense problems.[28] As Lady Bracknell says in Oscar Wilde's *The Importance of Being Earnest,* "The truth is never pure, and rarely simple."

A macabre tale is told of the god Moloch. He came down to earth to the premier of one of the new nations in Africa, with an offer: "I will provide you with a modern highway network if you will sacrifice 45,000 people to me every year." The premier, aghast, cried, "No! Not a single, solitary soul!" "Phooie," retorted Moloch, "that is what I get in the U.S.A. annually." Actuaries know in advance how many men will be killed for every fifty miles of new roads built or every ten floors of new buildings. By reducing the speed limit on our highways to fifteen miles an hour we could save more than four fifths of the lives that are lost in accidents. We don't do it, though. Why?

It is sentimental, simplistic, and romantically backward to "feel" that love cannot or ought not calculate; that it is either demeaned or diluted by having a memory, making future references, counting people, trying to figure the angles, finding its mix of alternatives and trying to win the game of optimum choice. Very much to the contrary, love grows up, is matured and actualized, when it permits

[27] Anatol Rapoport, *Fights, Games, and Debates* (University of Michigan Press, 1960).

[28] E.g., A. Rapoport, *Strategy and Conscience* (Harper & Row, Publishers, Inc., 1964).

a reasonable fire to warm its work but seeks more and more light, less and less heat. The heat it can leave to romance.

Love's business is not to play favorites or find friends or to "fall" for some one-and-only. It plays the field, universalizes its concern, has a social interest, is no respecter of persons. If we could ever claim (as Nygren did) that disinterested love is anything real at all, then it cannot mean that in such an ethic the lover is quite forgotten and only the loved remembered, i.e., that love is kenotic or self-emptying. Disinterested love can only mean impartial love, inclusive love, indiscriminate love, love for Tom, Dick, and Harry.

This is possible, such a disinterested love, because—as we say—*love wills the neighbor's good whether we like him or not.*

VII

Love Justifies Its Means

The Fifth Proposition: "Only the end justifies the means; nothing else."

WE GROW CYNICAL or despairing, depending on our temper, when we see the way Christian ethics down through the centuries has clung stubbornly to the doctrine that "the end does not justify the means." It is an absurd abstraction, equivalent to saying that a thing is not worth what it costs, that *nothing* is, that use or usefulness is irrelevant to price.

WHAT JUSTIFIES A MEANS?

In the perspective of situation ethics it is amazing that almost unanimously this sententious proposition has managed to hang on with bland and unchallenged acceptance. Just as Socrates saw that the unexamined life is not worth living, we can say that unexamined ethical maxims are not worth living by. Therefore we have to raise the question, implicit in all that has gone before, "If the end does not justify the means, what does?" The answer is, obviously, "Nothing!"

Unless some purpose or end is in view, to justify or sanctify it, any action we take is literally meaningless— i.e., means-less, accidental, merely random, pointless.

Every action without exception is haphazard if it is without an end to serve: it only acquires its status as a means, i.e., it only becomes meaningful by virtue of an end beyond itself. And ends, in their turn, need means. It has been suggested that there is a parallel here to Kant's saying about percepts and concepts; to paraphrase him, means without ends are empty and ends without means are blind. They are *relative* to each other. In any course of action it is the coexistence of its means and ends that puts it in the realm of ethics.

It is related in Soviet Russia how Nikolai Lenin once tired of being told by Tolstoyan idealists that his willingness to use force, in foreign and civil wars, proved that he had no ethics, that since violence *is* evil (not "can" be but *is*), and since his principles allowed him to use it, he therefore must believe that the end justifies the means. He finally rounded on them: "If the end does not justify the means, then in the name of sanity and justice, *what does?*" To this question he never got an answer—only open mouths and blank looks.

It should be plainly apparent, of course, that not any old end will justify any old means. We all assume that some ends justify some means; no situationist would make a universal of it! Being pragmatic, he always asks the price and supposes that in theory and practice everything has its price. *Everything*, please note. Even a "pearl of great price"—whatever it is—might be sold for love's sake if the situation calls for it.

If our loyalty goes more fully to the end we seek than to the means we use, as it should, then the means must be appropriate and faithful to the end. We ought not to forget Thomas Aquinas' warning that means are proximate ends, and that therefore the means we employ will enter into the end sought and reached, just as the flour and milk and raisins we use enter into the cake we bake. Means are ingredients, not merely neutral tools, and we

are called upon therefore to select them with the greatest
care. Means are not ethically indifferent. *In most situations* birth control by prevention, for example, is better
than abortion.

But it is equally evident, from the other side, that not
any old means is suitable to any old end. To recall A. C.
Ewing and H. R. Niebuhr's key term, the means used
ought to fit the end, ought to be *fitting*. If they are, they
are justified. For in the last analysis, it is the end sought
that gives the means used their meaningness. The end
does justify the means.

The classical moralists and pious popularizers have
tried, usually out of context, to absolutize and magnify
Paul's remark in Rom. 3:8: "And why not do evil that
good may come?" We say "magnify" because the remark
was made in the heat of controversy with the antinomians,
who were using human weakness and imperfection as a
reason for doing what they pleased, undisciplined. Paul
was certainly obscure and contradictory about the problem
of the justice of God. Could he justly condemn man's sin
if men are fated to sin and cannot of themselves escape it,
needing Christ to rescue them?

As Theodore Ferris says, it was a "confused wrangle"
in which Paul did "not provide a cogent answer to the
questions he raised."[1] He had seemed to the antinomians
to be saying that our sinful self-indulgence gives God a
chance to forgive us, which suited their purposes beau-
tifully! G. H. C. MacGregor argues that Paul's hecklers
wondered, therefore, "Why not be evil that good (grace)
may come?" and then adds, in a perfect piece of intrinsic
moralism, that this was an attempt to argue that evil is
good, "and *that* is nonsense."[2]

It *is* logical nonsense, at the verbal level, yes. To make

[1] *The Interpreter's Bible*, Nolan B. Harmon, ed., Vol. IX
(Abingdon Press, 1954), p. 423.
[2] *Ibid.*

the statement "Evil is good" is a formal violation of the rule of noncontradiction. But the real error in it, by which all of them are victimized (Paul, the antinomians, and MacGregor), is the intrinsic theory under which, logically, a thing is either good or evil. But good and evil are not properties, they are predicates or attributes. And *therefore* what is sometimes good may at other times be evil, and what is sometimes wrong may sometimes be right when it serves a good enough end—*depending on the situation.*

Law Entangles Itself

With its terrible literalism and legalism, classical Christian ethics has lent itself to a vast amount of equivocal and even downright contradictory opinion. Think of the endless debates and Talmudic pilpul ground out to rationalize those numerous things men have to do by means that are often unwelcome and sometimes tragic. They have always twisted and turned around their foolish doctrine that means are intrinsically good or evil, that they are not to be justified by any end or usefulness external to the supposedly inherent "value" of the means themselves. This pilpul has been ground out of the legalistic mills to rationalize war's ruthless methods of forcing, killing, lying, subverting, violating; it has strained to find moral reasons for capital and corporal punishment, diplomatic subterfuge, surgical mutilations, and a whole host of things.

The gyrations of formal moral theology around these questions result, of course, from an unlovely lip service paid to a maxim that the practices in question all *obviously* contradict! Surgeons have to mutilate bodies to remove cancers, some priests have to give up married love and children for their vocations' sake, nurses lie to schizophrenics to keep them calm for treatment. But in such cases it is *worth* it.

Every little book and manual on "problems of conscience" is legalistic. "Is it right to . . ." have premarital
intercourse, gamble, steal, euthanase, abort, lie, defraud,
break contracts, *et cetera, ad nauseum?* This kind of
intrinsicalist morass must be left behind as irrelevant,
incompetent; and immaterial. The new morality, situation
ethics, declares that anything and everything is right or
wrong, according to the situation. And this candid approach is indeed a revolution in morals! At the same time,
it is as ancient as the prophet Isaiah (ch. 4 : 1) who, fore-
seeing a day when the sex ratio would be imbalanced, said,
"Seven women shall take hold of one man" to even things
up. (With us, monogamy may be an ideal but it should
not be an idol.)

Alexander Miller interviewed some of the French
maquis after World War II, about their experiences in the
resistance struggle. (It is a famous passage in his *Renewal
of Man.*[3]) They had lived on lies (forged passports, ration
cards, I.D. cards, etc.), by theft of food and supplies, by
killing occupation officers and collaborators, sometimes
even killing one of their own members in danger of arrest
and exposing their whole conspiracy. He asked if everything, then, is permissible? Their reply was clear and
crucial. "Yes, everything is permitted—and everything is
forbidden." Miller's comment was that "if killing and
lying are to be used it must be under the most urgent
pressure of social necessity, and with a profound sense of
guilt that no better way can be presently found." We
should change his "guilt" to *sorrow,* since such tragic
situations are a cause for regret, but not for remorse. But
the main point is as he puts it.

Ponder this: Along the Wilderness Road, or Boone's
Trail, in the eighteenth century, westward through Cum-
berland Gap to Kentucky, many families and trail parties
lost their lives in border and Indian warfare. Compare
two episodes in which pioneers were pursued by savages.

[3] *The Renewal of Man,* pp. 99–100.

(1) A Scottish woman saw that her suckling baby, ill and crying, was betraying her and her three other children, and the whole company, to the Indians. But she clung to her child, and they were caught and killed. (2) A Negro woman, seeing how her crying baby endangered another trail party, killed it with her own hands, to keep silence and reach the fort. Which woman made the right decision?

We have already seen, in the discussion of our first proposition, that love only is always good, and that the intrinsic theory of value traps its holders into the untenable position of making absolute prohibitions of certain acts, regardless of the circumstances. Examples are telling a lie or committing suicide, when they could lead to a great deal of good. We also saw that intrinsicalism sometimes results in stigmatizing as a "lesser *evil*" such loving deeds as stealing a man's gun to keep him from shooting somebody in anger.

As Paul said twice in his first letter to Corinth (chs. 6:12 and 10:23), this intrinsic approach simply fails to grasp that it is not its being lawful that makes a thing good but only whether it is expedient, edifying, constructive—whether it builds up. Some sense of causation is essential to ethics, else we shall all be like the auto magnate who complained, "If these traffic jams didn't cause our workers to be late, we could make two hundred more cars each week."

What else could make a thing lawful, according to the only law left in the New Testament, i.e., Jesus' Summary? The answer is clear. Nothing. Nothing makes a thing good except agapeic expedience; nothing *can* justify an act except a loving purpose. Theodore Roosevelt was either not altogether honest (candid) or altogether thoughtful when he said, "No man is justified in doing evil on the ground of expediency."[4] He was mired down in intrin-

---

[4] *The Strenuous Life* (Century, 1901), quoted in ads of the Container Corporation of America.

sicalist legalism. Love could justify anything. There is no justification other than love's expedients. What else? In a particular case, why should not a single woman who could not marry become a "bachelor mother" by natural means or artificial insemination, even though husbandless, as a widow is?

Roosevelt's dogma calls even God's decisions into question, challenges God's ethical insight. According to some theologies, William Temple's and Josiah Royce's, for example, the problem of evil (how to explain its presence in a world created by a God who is both all-powerful and all-loving) is best resolved by the tutelage theory, the theory that God provides evil to drive men to rise to moral levels they would never reach without having to struggle and sacrifice and wrestle with evil.[5] Here is a theodicy based squarely on the view that the end justifies the means!

Once we realize and truly accept that only love is good in and of itself, and that no act apart from its foreseeable consequences has any *ethical* meaning whatsoever—only then will we see that the right question to ask is, Does an evil means always nullify a good end? And the answer, on a basis of what is sometimes called "due proportion," must be, "*No.*" It always depends upon the situation. When people oppose government lotteries because "gambling is wrong" they are petrified legalists; when they conclude against them as a policy carrying more evil than good, we can take them seriously—even if we do not agree.

We could, we might, decide that the whore in the Greek movie *Never on Sunday,* was right. In Piraeus near Athens she finds a young sailor who is afraid he cannot function sexually as an adult and virile man, and suffers as a prey to corrosive self-doubt and nonidentity. She

[5] Cf. Joseph Fletcher, *William Temple: Twentieth Century Christian* (The Seabury Press, Inc., 1963), pp. 80–82, 316–318.

manages things deliberately (i.e., responsibly) so that he
succeeds with her and gains his self-respect and psychic
freedom from a potential fixation on sex itself.

Look at the account written by an Episcopal priest in a
slum parish on the Eastern seaboard.[6] Trying to penetrate
the teen-agers' subculture, based on the structures of gang
or street-club organization, he arranged for the Knights
and their Debs to treat his church as home base. Faced
with frequent pregnancies in their pattern of sexual prom-
iscuity, he raised the question with them whether, if they
would not be chaste, they ought not to use contraceptives.

He found, not surprisingly, that they were ignorant of
such matters. Disease, illegal abortions, bastardy reigned.
But did he help them, in spite of what he calls the "very
wide chasm" between their behavior standards and his
church's? *He says not a word about this,* and one fears
that his silence is not discretion but an implicit admission
that legalistic "idealism" cut him off from a loving decision
to help them. (Legalistic puritanism has also prevented
relief agencies from helping client-mothers to use contraceptives, thus adding enormously to relief costs, on the
ground that a promiscuous woman *and her children*
should suffer for her sins.)

THE FOUR FACTORS

And what is it, then, that we are to take into account as
we analyze and weigh and judge the situation? What do
we look for, what question do we ask? There are four
questions of basic and indispensable importance to be
raised about every case, four factors at stake in every
situation, all of which are to be balanced on love's scales.
There are no foregone decisions.

The first one, the primary one, is the *end.* What is

[6] C. K. Myers, *Light the Dark Streets* (The Seabury Press,
Inc., 1957), pp. 46–48.

wanted? What is the object sought; what result is aimed
at? A student, for example, might want a new and highly
useful thesaurus. But then, as a second factor, by what
means could he acquire one; what method should he
employ to bring about the end he seeks? It might be stealing or borrowing or buying, and to get money to buy it he
might steal or save or beg or borrow or gamble. This, then,
brings into view the third factor at stake, his *motive*.
What is the drive or "wanting" dynamic behind the act?
Is the student moved by covetousness or charity or scholarship or ostentation or bibliomania?

Finally, every serious decision maker needs to ask the
fourth question, What are the foreseeable *consequences*?
Given any course of action, in the context of the problem,
what are the effects directly and indirectly brought about,
the immediate consequences, and the remote (sequelae)?
This last question means, we must note, that there are
more results entailed than just the end wanted, and they
all have to be weighed and weighted. Along with getting
the thesaurus, there may come other things: impoverishment, a neurosis nurtured, professional growth, resent-
ment by a wife or creditor, successful completion of an
important thesis.

Rigoristic, intrinsicalist legalism often takes the position
that to be wrong an action need be at fault on only one
of these four scores, whereas in order to be right it must
be right on *all four*. When Kant, the grandfather of
modern ethical absolutizers, wrote his essay *On a Supposed
Right to Tell Lies from Benevolent Motives,* he made it
quite clear that in his ethics a lie to a would-be murderer,
to save his victims' life, would be wrong. The situationist
prefers the ethics of the civil law, in which the failure
to tell the necessary lie might very possibly make one an
accessory before the fact of the murder!

Here we are up against universals and the categorical
imperative, once more. But we recognize no imperatives
at all except *hypothetical* ones: i.e., an action is imperative

only if the situation demands it for love's sake. Schopenhauer once said that whether Kant called his legalistic
absolutism "the categorical imperative" or "fitziputzli," it
was still "the drill-sergeant theology of eighteenth-century
Prussia with the drill-sergeant turned into an abstraction."[7]
He rightly called it the "apotheosis of lovelessness, the
exact opposite, as it is, of the Christian doctrine of
morals."[8]

Ever since Chrysostom's day it has been said that the
essence of sin lies in the confusion of means with ends.
When a thing becomes an end in itself, as money does
with a miser, rather than a means to some personal good
as its proper end, there is sin. If narcotic euphoria is sought
as an end in itself, rather than as a means to analgesia or
mental healing (opium-morphine addicts do this), that
is sin. But it is of special importance here to emphasize
from the situationist's angle of vision, that *ends,* like
means, are relative, that all ends and means are related
to each other in a contributory hierarchy, and that *in
their turn* all ends become means to some end higher than
themselves. There is only one end, one goal, one purpose
which is not relative and contingent, always an end in
itself. Love.

This is worth stressing. *Not only means but ends too are
relative,* only extrinsically justifiable. They are good only
if they happen to contribute to some good other than
themselves. Nothing is intrinsically good but the highest
good, the *summum bonum,* the end or purpose of all ends
—love. We cannot say anything we do *is* good, only that
it is a means to an end and therefore *happens* in that
cause-and-effect relation to have value.

Bishop Kirk came close to an extrinsic, situational view
when, speaking of the old rule about means and ends, he
said, "The correct form of the maxim, in fact, is 'circum-

[7] Arthur Schopenhauer, *The Basis of Morality,* tr. by A. B.
Bullock (The Macmillan Company, 1903), p. 50.

[8] *Ibid.,* p. 6.

stances alter cases.' And this is obviously true. An act
which is right in some circumstances may be wrong in
others."[9] But he only came close; he did not, alas, say
(as he should have) that an act which is *wrong* in some
cases would be right in others. He failed to reach home
because he acknowledged only one side of the coin. His
bid for freedom from legalism was too fainthearted.

There are those who invoke the "wedge" principle
against any attempt to weigh relative values. Exceptions
to a law are a dangerous wedge, a camel's nose in the tent,
they say. Euthanasia, for example, is said to be "an act
which, if raised to a general line of conduct would injure
humanity, [and] is wrong in the individual case."[10] A particular case of loving-kindness, *if everybody did it,* would
mean chaos or cruelty.

Legalists argue that the consequence of disobeying law,
moral or civil, is that it weakens law and order and that
the "ultimate" result "would be" anarchy, no matter how
desirable the immediate consequences. An English court
recently gave the lightest possible prison sentence to a
father convicted of ending the life of a Mongolian idiot
son, on the ground that although the judge might have
done the same thing in those circumstances, to let him
escape the law and penalties of murder would encourage
others to commit murder and weaken the social fabric.

At first sight this looks like a realistic awareness that
there are remote as well as immediate consequences to be
taken into account in every decision. But actually it is only
another disguise for Kant's abstract rule that every act in
order to be moral must be *universally* willed. There is no
human act, no matter how lovingly willed, which could
not lead to evil if the circumstances were of a certain

[9] *The Study of Theology* (London: Hodder & Stoughton,
Ltd., 1939), p. 383.

[10] J. V. Sullivan, *Catholic Teaching on the Morality of
Euthanasia* (Catholic University Press, 1949), p. 54.

pattern—and to say "universal only for exactly similar conditions" is to run away from the variety of life.

The wedge is very much like reactionary objections to new increases in our human control over the conditions of life. If we allow the use of contraceptives, it is said, people will selfishly stop having children. (Often it will stop people stupidly having children!) The adequate answer is *Abusus non tollit usum* (Abuse does not bar use).

The wedge is not used, obviously, against our having executioners for capital punishment, or soldiers, or celibates. The "generalization argument" (What would happen if everybody did it?) is actually one of the maneuvers used to discredit personal responsibility and leave law in control. It is a fundamentally antisituational gambit. It is a form of obstructionism, a delaying action of static morality.

Hallowing the Means

However you decide your choices, the end justifies the means. It certainly cannot justify itself. Furthermore, the only self-validating end in the Christian situation ethic is love. All other ends and *all* means are justified according to the changes and chances of unlimitedly diverse situations.

What has often been quoted as a proof of the Jesuits' double-dealing and evasion of the "moral law" is, in fact, to their credit; we embrace their maxim wholeheartedly: *Finis sanctificat media* (The end justifies or sanctifies or validates the means). This is precisely what our principle of extrinsic or contingent value leads to. Brunner put it in much the same fashion, that "the necessary end sanctifies the necessary means."[11] Therefore he could speak of "the hallowing of the means by the end." (N. H. Søe of Denmark said of Brunner, "He never turned out to be a

[11] *The Divine Imperative*, p. 246.

Situationsethiker." But all the evidence says that Søe is mistaken.[12])

It is a snare and a delusion to think that we can escape doubts and conflicts by turning to law. One legalist moralist has written of a captured spy's problem, "Direct suicide would constitute a bad means to a good end, even though he fears to divulge vital information through coercion and torture. The same case would occur if a priest feared that he is to be tortured in order to force him to break the sacramental seal. He should pray for strength to be silent, but he may not commit suicide."[13] Here we see a head-on collision between the absolute of life (not so much of its preservation as of its nonsacrifice!) and the absolute of secrecy.

The same kind of "perplexity" arises for legalism when the conflict is between the rule of secrecy and the demands of love-justice, when a priest learns "under the seal" that an innocent man is about to die for the penitent's crime. Canon law forbids him to reveal what he knows. Why is the spy's life more important than the lives of his fellow countrymen? Why is the priest's seal more sacrosanct than the life of the luckless victim of circumstances, waiting in death row? (It would seem that self-preservation comes first, then keeping the seal inviolate, and a poor third is neighbor-love!)

Therefore, in the relativities of this world where conscience labors to do the right thing, we may always do what would be evil in some contexts if in *this* circumstance love gains the balance. It is love's business to calculate gains and losses, and to act for the sake of its success.

On this ground, then, we must flatly oppose the classical means-ends rule in Christian ethics and moral theology.

[12] *The Theology of Emil Brunner,* ed. by C. W. Kegley (The Macmillan Company, 1962), p. 255.

[13] F. J. Connell, in *American Ecclesiastical Review,* Vol. CXLII (1960), pp. 132–133.

We have to refuse to omit doing a preponderantly good deed just because the necessary means happens to be evil "generally" or because it entails some evil. For us, whether it is good or evil, right or wrong, is not *in* the deed but *by* its circumstances. William James liked to say that truth does not exist *ante rem,* before or apart from the facts as lived, but *in rebus*—in the lived event itself. And so with the good! Several years ago Congress passed a special bill giving citizenship to a Roumanian Jewish doctor, a woman, who had aborted three thousand Jewish women brought to the concentration camp. If pregnant, they were to be incinerated. Even accepting the view that the embryos were "human lives" (which many of us do not), by "killing" three thousand the doctor saved three thousand and prevented the murder of *six thousand!*

If, for example, the emotional and spiritual welfare of the parents and children in a *particular* family could best be served by a divorce, then, wrong and cheap-jack as divorce often is, love justifies a divorce. Love's method is to judge by particularity, not to lay down laws and universals. It does not preach pretty propositions; it asks concrete questions, situation questions. Getting a divorce is sometimes like David's eating the reserved Sacrament; it is what Christ would recommend. The fact that Jesus is reported in the Gospels as having blessed David's act on the basis of the situation, while he also absolutized the prohibition of divorce, poses a problem for Biblical scholarship (especially troublesome to the literalizers and legalists) but it does not confuse Christian ethics, at least of the situationist stamp. We are quite clear about it: to will the end is to will the means.

Only the end justifies the means: nothing else.

VIII

Love Decides There and Then

The Sixth Proposition: "Love's decisions are made situationally, not prescriptively."

SOMETIMES EXECUTIVES WITH a taste for irony exhibit a comic desk sign which reads, "My Mind Is Made Up, Don't Confuse Me with the Facts!" It is a sad bit of humor because it points a finger at a fatal yet widespread form of spiritual and moral insecurity.

WANTED: A SYSTEM

Too many people at heart long for an ethical *system* of prefabricated, pretailored morality. They want to lean on strong, unyielding rules. It was all very well, they complain, for Paul to say that living by law is like slavery (Gal. 4:21–26), "but after all, *we* aren't St. Pauls." Even if he did say that those who stick to the law are no better than slaves, we still need law—and if not the Torah, then something like it, something more "Christian."

People like to wallow or cower in the security of the law. They cannot trust themselves too much to the freedom of grace; they prefer the comfortableness of law. Better the policy of the Grand Inquisitor; better bread and circuses. If, as the philosophers say, man became "the tragic animal" by transcending instinctually determined choices and acquiring conscience, then it's at least better to keep that tragic burden of conscience to a safe minimum! In a way they are right; moving over from law to love (Paul called it "grace") is a painful and threatening step to take.

The situationist, cutting himself loose from the dead hand of unyielding law, with its false promises of relief from the anguish of decision, can only determine that as a man of goodwill he will live as a free man, with all the ambiguities that go along with freedom. His moral life takes on the shape of adventure, ceases to pretend to be a blueprint. In all humility, knowing that he cannot escape the human margin of error, he will—in Luther's apposite phrase—sin bravely.

THE GRAY AREA

When we wrestle with real problems of conscience, not easy or obvious ones, we are in "the ethical penumbra"— where things are not too certain. In between the brightly lighted side of a satellite, where the sun's light reaches, and the dark side turned away (the umbra), lies the shadowed, partly lighted area in between, the penumbra. So many decisions in life are of this kind; they fall in between. This "penumbric" concern of situation ethics is parallel to Bonhoeffer's penultimate concern with history and the world.[1] It meets things here and now, without a romantic focus on the past or an escapist focus on the future.

This is where the call to sin bravely is sharpest. When a lady in Arizona learned, a few years ago, that she *might* bear a defective baby because she had taken thalidomide, how was she to decide? She asked the court to back her doctor and his hospital in terminating the pregnancy, and it refused, to the judge's chagrin, since the law prohibits

[1] *Ethics*, pp. 84 ff.

nonmedically indicated abortions without exception. Her husband took her to Sweden, where love has more control of law, and there she was aborted. God be thanked, since the embryo was hideously deformed. But nobody could know for sure. It was a brave and responsible and right decision, even if the embryo had been all right. It was a *kairos,* a fullness of time, a moment of decision.

In 1841 the ship *William Brown,* out of Liverpool for Philadelphia, struck an iceberg off Newfoundland and began to sink. Two boats got away; the captain, some of the crew, and a passenger in one were picked up after six days. The other, the longboat, was in charge of the first mate. He, seven seamen, and thirty-two passengers were twice what it could hold. Rain and rough seas doomed them. The mate ordered most of the males into the sea; they refused and Holmes, a seamen, pitched them out. The rest were finally picked up. In Philadelphia, Holmes was convicted of murder, mercy recommended.[2] Regardless of the *kairos,* says legalism, Holmes did an evil thing, not a good thing. Situation ethics says it was bravely sinful, it was a good thing.

When Captain Scott's expedition to the South Pole ran into trouble and they were making it back to the coast with no time to spare, one of his men was injured and had to be carried. The stretcher would slow them dangerously. Scott decided to stick with the man, not abandon him, and they all perished. But it was an authentic *kairos,* and assuming Scott was not simply legalistic in his decision, it does him as much honor as Holmes's or the Arizona lady's. We can't always guess the future, even though we are always being forced to try.

This contextual, situational, clinical case method (or neocasuistry), this way of dealing with decision, is too full of variables to please some people. They like better to latch on to a few well-anchored constants, sanctioned in law,

[2] See Edmund Cahn, *The Moral Decision* (Indiana University Press, 1956), pp. 61–71.

and ignore all the variables. That is law's way. But it is not love's way. And added to this difference, which has always existed, is the further fact that life and culture in a technical civilization is becoming increasingly complicated, either very specialized or very wide-scoped and interdisciplinary, so that ethical problem-solving and decision-making are growing knottier all the time, with the "gray area" between the black and white spreading. Through the increase of professional expertise and special knowledge, perfectionism is being banished progressively from Christian ethics; and, for the same reason, petty moralism is forced to come of age and to face the complicated facts of life.

Under the pressures and revelations of the "information explosion" in this era, prefab code morality gets exposed as a kind of neurotic security device to simplify moral decisions. It may be, on some balanced view, that true order presupposes freedom and freedom presupposes order, but just the same, it is the *order* that looms largest in the legalist's eye.

THE END OF IDEOLOGY

Political and social establishments feel safer when buttressed by an ethical establishment, a fixed code. In some circles there is a growing hunger for law; it can be seen in cultural conformism, and in the lust for both political and theological orthodoxy. Like the existentialists to an extent, situationists are in revolt against the cultural stodginess of "respectable" and traditional ethics. They rebel against the reigning ethics of American middle-class culture because of its high-flown moral laws on the one hand and its evasive shilly-shallying on the other; it is often and acutely described as "the leap from Sunday to Monday."

Nothing in the world causes so much conflict of conscience as the continual, conventional payment of lip service to moral "laws" that are constantly flouted in practice because they are too petty or too rigid to fit the facts of life. Many people prefer to fit reality to rules rather than to fit rules to reality. Legalism always bears down hard on the need for order, putting its premium on obedience to law, even statutory law. It would, if it could, immobilize Martin Luther King and the sit-in demonstrators or civil rights protesters, whereas situation ethics gives high-order value to freedom, and to that *responsibility* for free decision which is the obverse side of the coin of freedom.

In ethics as in politics we can see that ideology has come to a dead end. Doctrinaire by-the-book theory and practice is too confining, too narrow. "The point is," says Daniel Bell, "that ideologists are terrible simplifiers. Ideology makes it unnecessary for people to confront individual issues in individual situations. One simply turns to the ideological vending machine, and out comes the prepared formula."[3] Substitute "law" for ideology in Bell's statement and we have the nub of the matter. A committee set up by the late President Kennedy to deal with questions of business ethics, of which the writer of this book was a member, got nowhere at all because it was code-minded, wrote a code to cover all business, and found itself possessed of nothing but platitudes.

For real decision-making, freedom is required, an open-ended approach to situations. Imagine the plight of an obstetrician who believed he must always respirate every baby he delivered, no matter how monstrously deformed! A century ago Thomas Huxley rather thought he would prefer being accurate and correct as a moral decision maker, even if he had to be as mechanical as a clock wound up for the day, than assume the burden of mistakes entailed by freedom. What an irony to compare his opinion to Tik-Tok's in *The Wizard of Oz*! There the mechanical

[3] *The End of Ideology: On the Exhaustion of Political Ideas in the Fifties,* new rev. ed. (Collier Books, 1962), p. 17.

man had the special grace of always doing "what he was wound up to do," but wanted instead to be *human*. And what did he lack? Freedom to choose.

No wonder that Jesus, in the language of a French Catholic moralist whose concern is contemporary, "reacted particularly against code morality and against casuistry," and that his "attitude toward code morality [was] purely and simply one of reaction."[4] Modern Christians ought not to be naïve enough to accept any other view of Jesus' ethic than the situational one. When Edmund Wilson ran his famous article in *The New Yorker* some ten years ago on the Dead Sea Scrolls he made quite a splash by saying that Jesus' teaching was a copy of the Essenes' teaching at the Qumran community.[5] Actually, the quickest way to expose the error in all such uncritical comparisons is simply to point out that the legalism and code rule of the Qumran sect put even the Pharisees to shame, whereas Jesus boldly rejected all such legalisms.

As we know, for many people, sex is so much a moral problem, largely due to the repressive effects of legalism, that in newspapers and popular parlance the term "morals charge" always means a sex complaint! "Her morals are not very high" means her sex life is rather looser than the mores allow. Yet we find nothing in the teachings of Jesus about the ethics of sex, except adultery and an absolute condemnation of divorce—a correlative matter. He said nothing about birth control, large or small families, childlessness, homosexuality, masturbation, fornication or premarital intercourse, sterilization, artificial insemination, abortion, sex play, petting, and courtship. Whether any form of sex (hetero, homo, or auto) is good or evil depends on whether love is fully served.

[4] J. LeClercq, *Christ and the Modern Conscience*, pp. 59, 61.

[5] Republished as *The Scrolls from the Dead Sea* (Oxford University Press, 1955).

The Christian ethic is not interested in reluctant virgins and technical chastity. What sex probably needs more than anything is a good airing, demythologizing it and getting rid of its mystique-laden and occult accretions, which come from romanticism on the one hand and puritanism on the other. People are learning that we can have sex without love, and love without sex; that baby-making can be (and often ought to be) separated from love-making. It is, indeed, for re-creation as well as for procreation. But if people do not believe it is wrong to have sex relations outside marriage, it isn't, unless they hurt themselves, their partners, or others. This is, of course, a very big "unless" and gives reason to many to abstain altogether except within the full mutual commitment of marriage. The civil lawmakers are rapidly ridding their books of statutes making unmarried sex a crime between consenting adults. All situationists would agree with Mrs. Patrick Campbell's remark that they can do what they want "as long as they don't do it in the street and frighten the horses."

Situation ethics always suspects prescriptive law of falsifying life and dwarfing moral stature, whether it be the Scripture legalism of Biblicist Protestants and Mohammedans or the nature legalism (natural law) of the Catholics and disciples of Confucius. One American theologian has complained that situation ethics fails to realize that people are unwilling to grapple with what he calls "paradoxical ambiguities"—that they want something more definite and exact than ethical relativism offers.[6] Of course; they want the Grand Inquisitor. T. S. Eliot was right to say that people cannot bear too much reality. But there is no escape for them. To learn love's sensitive tactics, such people are going to have to put away their childish rules.

[6] W. Burnett Easton, Jr., "Ethical Relativism and Popular Morality," *loc. cit.*

FANATIC VIRTUE

As the old adage has it, "Virtue never goes out of style," i.e., the *disposition* toward honor, chastity, loyalty, patience, humility, and all the rest. But *situations* change. There is another old saying, *Semper sed non ad semper* (Principles are always sound but not in every case). What is constructive in one era may not be in another; James Russell Lowell's hymn is right, "Time makes ancient good uncouth." Humility and gentility once meant that women should be ignoramuses, but it doesn't anymore! As Raymond Bruckberger, a French priest and student of American culture, puts it, "Fanatic love of virtue has done more to damage men and society than all the vices put together."[7]

Who could ever forget that "virtue" can serve the devil, after seeing Henrik Ibsen's *The Wild Duck*? Young Gregers Werle did far more harm to far more people than his lying father had, simply by telling the truth about the past, thereby destroying a girl, her mother and father, his own father. And Dr. Relling, the situationist, alone protested that the truth must not be told, for love's sake. In every milieu we have to know and to calculate. It is entirely possible to be calculating without being loving, but it is *not* possible to be loving without calculating.

If it is true, as under the New Testament rubric, Jesus' Summary, that actions are only right *because* they are loving, it follows that they are only right *when* or while or as long as they are loving! The righteousness of an act (i.e., its rightness) does not reside in the act itself, but holistically *in its* Gestalt, *in the loving configuration*, the aggregate, whole complex of all the factors in the situation, the total context.

Theology or theologizing is *done* at the point of en-

[7] *Image of America* (The Viking Press, Inc., 1959), p. 64.

counter between faith and life, church and world. Tillich has insisted that true theology arises where a question in the situation is posed and calls for an answer from the "message," making for a situational theology. In the same way true ethics arises where a situation poses questions. What Tillich calls the method of correlation applies to all of theology, moral as well as doctrinal.

As the Christian situationist sees it, his faith answers for him three questions of the seven always to be asked. These three are his "universals." He knows the *what;* it is love. He knows the *why;* for God's sake. He knows the *who;* it is his neighbors, people. But only in and of the situation can he answer the other four questions: When? Where? Which? How? These are, as we have suggested, the *kairos* factors. There and then only can he find out what is the right thing to do. The Christian ethic is a love ethic primarily, not a hope ethic (although it has its eschatalogical meaning). This means it is for the present, here and now. By faith we live in the past, by hope we live in the future, but by love we live in the *present.*[8] Legalism is wrong because it tries to push love back into the past, into old decisions already made.

Ecology is the study of the relation between an organism and its environment. We may say, then, that situation ethics is an ecological ethics, for it takes as full account as possible of the context (environment) of every moral decision. This means looking carefully at the full play of ends, means, motives, and result. The rightness is in the *Gestalt* or shape of the action as a whole, and not in any single factor or ingredient.

Is adultery wrong? To ask this is to ask a mare's-nest question. It is a glittering generality, like Oscar Wilde's mackerel in the moonlight: it glitters but it stinks. One can only respond, "I don't know. Maybe. Give me a case.

[8] Cf. Emil Brunner, *Faith, Hope and Love* (The Westminster Press, 1956), p. 13.

Describe a real situation." Or perhaps somebody will ask
if a man should ever lie to his wife, or desert his family,
or spy on a business rival's design or market plans, or fail
to report some income item in his tax return. Again, the
answer cannot be an answer, it can only be another
question. "Have you a *real* question, that is to say, a
concrete situation?" If it has to do with premarital sex or
libel or breach of contract or anything else ("you name
it"), the reply is always the same: "You are using words,
abstractions. What you are asking is without substance;
it has no living reality. There is no way to answer such
questions."

Here we are in direct opposition to the detachment of
the mystics and abstractions of metaphysics, to be seen for
what they are in a Buddhist sutra: "Our mind should
stand aloof from circumstances, and on no account should
we allow them to influence the function of our mind."[9]
Nicolas Berdyaev may have been less than coherent at
many points, but at least he saw clearly that contrary to
the generalizers, "every moral action should have in view
a concrete living person and not the abstract good."[10]

WHEN RIGHTS ARE RIGHT

When love reigns, not law, the decisions of conscience
are relative. Love plots the course according to the circumstances. What is to be done in any situation depends on
the case, and the solution of any moral issue is, therefore,
quite relative. What is right is revealed in the facts: *Ex
factis oritur jus.* But once the relative course is chosen, the
obligation to pursue it is absolute. We cannot blow hot or
cold, or lukewarm, sounding an uncertain note about the

[9] Sutra of Wei Lang, quoted in C. Humphreys, *Buddhism*
(Penguin Books, Inc., 1952), p. 17.
[10] *The Destiny of Man* (Charles Scribner's Sons, 1960),
p. 106.

obligation itself. The obligation is absolute; only the decision is relative. Only the *how* is relative, not the *why*.
This is why we have said that the task is "to find absolute
love's relative course."

The metaphysical moralist of the classical tradition,
with his intrinsic values and moral universals and code
apparatus, says in effect, "Do what is right and let the
chips fall where they may." The situational decision
maker says right back at his metaphysical rival: "Ha!
Whether what you are doing is right or not depends precisely upon where the chips fall." Only the unwary will be
taken in by the pseudobravery and bogus prophetic courage
of those who drive ahead to an ideal regardless of the
pain or price involved. It is right or wrong to follow a
principle only according to who gets hurt, and how much.

John Kasper, a racist agitator and anti-Negro dema-
gogue, was convicted in a Tennessee court of inciting to
riot because of his activity in resisting school integration
in Clinton, in east Tennessee. Kasper appealed to the
First Amendment on a personal liberty and free-speech
basis. But in his instructions to the jury, Judge Homer
Weimer pointed out that while we all have a right to
make public speeches, we all have an obligation to calculate the consequences for the general welfare. A Christian
situationist, sitting on the bench, might have said to
Kasper, "You may claim a 'natural' or 'God-given' or con-
stitutional right to speak, if you want, but whether you
have *a right to exercise your right,* i.e., whether you have
a right at all in the situation, depends—it all depends."

Using classical terms, which even a situationist can do
honestly, the juridical order never exactly coincides with
the moral order. They never manage to reach a true "fit,"
and the moral order, with love in the driver's seat, always
takes first place whenever the fit is lacking. Love can
even love law, if law knows its place and takes the back
seat. Legal rights are subordinate, and so are legal prohibi-

tions. Under Aristotelian influence, classical Roman Catholic moral theology has tended to treat love as the "form" and law as the "matter," regarding them as coinherent and inseparable. But in the situationists' view such an ontological metaphysic only misreads and misdirects love and law. For although law may sometimes be the matter of love, there are other times when law denies love and destroys it. The core difference, however, is that *love's decisions are made situationally, not prescriptively.*

IX

Postscriptum: Why?

WHAT ARE WE to say now of the girl in our first chapter who was offered so much money to sleep with a rich man? Now that we have covered the ground in between, how shall we respond to the question whether extramarital sex is always wrong? Or even *paid* sex? Women have done it to feed their families, to pay debts, to serve their countries in counterespionage, to honor a man whom they could not marry. Are we not entitled to say that, depending on the situation, those who break the Seventh Commandment of the old law, even whores, *could* be doing a good thing —*if* it is for love's sake, for the neighbor's sake? In short, is there any real "law" of universal weight? The situationist thinks not.

A NEOCASUISTRY

The *Situations-ethik* more and more openly wins a place in nonfundamentalist Protestant ethics. It is sparking or cultivating a kind of neocasuistry. Occasionally leading Protestant writers take issue with the relativism of the method, but this appears to be a *mood* objection rather than genuinely critical. Two such moralists in America, John Bennett and Daniel Williams, have made the mistake of thinking that the situational method *procedurally* is antinomian, and that it works without any principles at all.[1] But, they say, they have no quarrel with it *substantively*. Compared to the right-wing Evangelicals and their antisituational posture, employing such epithets as "moral nihilism" and "sneaky minimalism," there is an imposing array of American Protestant moralists in the situational camp.[2] None has appeared without running into bad weather in the Roman communion yet, but Bernhard Häring, C.Ss.R., and Gerard Gilleman, S.J., have come a long way toward putting love at the ethical helm instead of nature, and personalism rather than legalism gives the work of many others a situational quality heretofore absent. There are many nontheological ethicists who do not consciously theorize as situationists, but that is what they are in actual practice. It may well be, on careful thought, that in effect most men are situationists and always have been!

yes, I think so.

Situationism, it appears, is the crystal precipitated in Christian ethics by our era's pragmatism and relativism. Historically, most men really have been situationists, more or less, but the difference today is that we are situationists as a matter of rational and professed method. Gone is the old legalistic sense of guilt and of cheated ideals when we tailor our ethical cloth to fit the back of each occasion. We are deliberately closing the gap between our overt professions and our covert practices. It is an age of honesty, this age of anxiety is.

All of this "new morality" is a neocasuistry. G. E. Moore said in his *Principia Ethica* that "casuistry is the goal of ethical investigation," but if one is quite wholeheartedly a situationist, he will insist that we begin with cases, too,

[1] Bennett, "Ethical Principles and the Context," unpublished presidential address, American Society of Christian Ethics, 1961; Williams, *What Present-Day Theologians Are Thinking*, rev. ed. (Harper & Brothers, 1959), pp. 114 ff.

[2] See the superb survey by J. M. Gustafson, "Christian Ethics," *loc. cit.*, pp. 285–354.

empirically. This neocasuistry is, like classical casuistry, case-focused and concrete, concerned to bring Christian imperatives into practical operation. But unlike classical casuistry, this neocasuistry repudiates the attempt to anticipate or prescribe real-life decisions in their existential particularity. The Christian conscience is not a vending machine, with handles to pull and prepackaged answers to spew out of a slot. As Whitehead remarked, "The simpleminded use of the notions 'right or wrong' is one of the chief obstacles to the progress of understanding."[3] We have to make a new effort to appreciate what Brunner calls, as we have noted, "the occasionalism of love."

Looking back in the history of Christian ethics from this vantage point, we can see that there is, after all, no discredit to the old-fashioned casuists, nor to the Talmudists, in the old saying that they continually made new rules for the breaking of old rules. They were pulling out of the nets or traps of their own precepts and principles, trying desperately to serve love as well as law. Inevitably the only result was a never-ending tangle of legalism. Code law always fails in the end to be corrected in favor of loving kindness. The rabbis throttled *hesed* and *zaddik*, the canonists strangled *agapē*. They simply and foolishly forgot that it is love which is the constitutive principle—and that law, at most, is only the regulative principle, if it is even that. Even today, in spite of a revival of Biblical theology, three difficulties about an agapeic ethic remain: (1) People do not understand the concept itself; (2) it is resisted philosophically and ethically even when it *is* understood; and (3) it is not central in Christian church teaching despite its centrality in the New Testament.

It must be confessed that the neocasuists do not always render justice to the classical casuistry. For example, Edward LeRoy Long confuses the old casuistry with com-

[3] A. N. Whitehead, *Modes of Thought* (The Macmillan Company, 1938), p. 15.

promise.[4] This is a serious error because the old moralists were always careful to stress that their solutions of problems of doubt and perplexity involved no compromise of principles and precepts, but rather their proper ordering. The old casuistry was not motivated by any desire to cut corners or to water the milk. Nor was Dietrich Bonhoeffer entirely correct when he identified what he called ethical "formalism" with casuistry.[5] Bonhoeffer's discussion reflected a great deal of confusion about casuistry, just as Karl Barth's does in his *Church Dogmatics*.[6]

As a matter of fact, Bonhoeffer's own plea for the necessity of being "concrete" and his treatment in the excursus on "What Is Meant by 'Telling the Truth' " in his *Ethics* is as radical a version of the situational method as any Christian relativist could call for. He has the heart of the matter, at least: "Law always engenders lawlessness; nomism leads to antinomism; perfectionism to libertinism."[7] And so with Barth, who says quite succinctly, "There is a practical casuistry, an active casuistry, the casuistry of the prophetic ethos. It consists in the unavoidable venture . . . of understanding God's concrete specific command here and now."[8] We have already seen that Brunner, a third "Big B" of modern theology, saw not only the core truth of situationism (which he called "occasionalism") but also its vitality and creative power in the lives of men.

Theological moralists such as Bonhoeffer and Barth and Brunner are, in any case, clearheaded and plainspoken about the central thesis of situation ethics, i.e., the absoluteness of the word of love and the relativity of the deed,

---

[4] *Conscience and Compromise: An Outline of Protestant Casuistry* (The Westminster Press, 1954).

[5] E.g., *Ethics*, p. 258.

[6] E.g., *Church Dogmatics*, Vol. III, Bk. 4, pp. 7–8.

[7] *Ethics*, p. 66.

[8] *Church Dogmatics*, Vol. III, Bk. 4, p. 9.

and their recognition that the total context of decision is always "circumstances under the law of love." Their mistake, which is even so not a serious one, is their lack of historical sophistication. To cite but one theory among Christian moral systems which are very close in temper to what we are proposing, there are the principles of so-called "compensationism." Two are most pointed for our purpose. Stodgy and system-oriented as the compensationists were (e.g., Dominic Prümmer), they made it their rule in complex cases (1) to do their ethical choosing between alternative courses according to the concrete and individuating particulars; and (2) to choose the course productive of the greater good. This method, which they called "the system of sufficient reason," they put in the place of probabilism and probabiliorism. They even accepted the label, "the moral system of Christian prudence." But it was always to be a "natural" prudence that bowed obediently to the authority of "supernatural" love, not the other way around.

No More Tablets of Stone

Our modern situational approach to ethical decisions has a fundamental parallel in the ancient world, in the *epieikeia* (or *epikeia,* as the medieval writers wrote it), i.e., equity. It was conceptualized by Aristotle and, following him, by Aquinas in his *Summa.*[9] Kenneth Kirk called it "a just interpretation of the law with due reference to the circumstances of the particular case."[10] The Jesuit Henry Davis quoted Aristotle's ancient description of *epikeia:* "Equity makes allowance for human weakness, looking not to the law but to the meaning of the lawgiver, not to the act but to the intention, not to the part but to the whole."[11] Luther saw it (*epieikeia, aequitas, clementia,*

[9] *Summa Theologica,* ii.2, q. 120, a.1.

[10] *Some Principles,* p. 208n.

[11] *Moral and Pastoral Theology* (Sheed & Ward, Inc., 1935), Vol. I, p. 187.

commoditas) as the spirit of the love ethic facing law and concrete situations.[12] This is how any person-centered ethic "condenses" into guidance insights in particular cases.[13]

Here, in classical paganism, are the same accents we find in Paul's affirmation of the spirit rather than the letter of law; it is what governs the bench in every serious court of equity. Pagan and secular ethics put to shame many Christian legalists, who refuse to apply equity to either their "natural" or their "divine" law, holding that God is the author of nature's laws or of certain tablets of stone bearing divine decrees by fiat, and that God's prescience has foreseen every situation!

Christian situation ethics, the "nonsystem" advocated here, has a critically shrewd tactical formula for the strategy of love: *The indicative plus the imperative equals the normative.* Love, in the imperative mood of neighbor-concern, examining the relative facts of the situation in the indicative mood, discovers what it is obliged to do, what it should do, in the normative mood. What is, in the light of what love demands, shows what ought to be.

(The two older Niebuhrs, Reinhold at Union and Helmut Richard at Yale, have made deep marks on Christian ethics in America. Each has in his own way contributed. But from the point of view of situation ethics, with its stress on responsible decisions, it is Helmut Richard's work that will be permanent. Reinhold's massive emphasis on man's "fallen" nature was sobering and gave a needed corrective at a certain time; he shocked perfectionist Protestant idealism with its detheologized posture, the "social gospel." But his brother's stress on the responsible self, his reaffirmation of the prophetic conviction

[12] William Lazareth, *Luther on the Christian Home* (Muhlenberg Press, 1960), p. 122.
[13] W. G. Maclagan, "Respect for Persons as a Moral Principle," in *Philosophy*, Vol. 35 (1960), pp. 193–217, 289–305.

that men *can* respond to the love of God—this is the creative and enduring thing. And it is a linchpin in Christian situation ethics.)

Said Paul to the saints at Philippi: "And this I pray, that your love may abound yet more and more in knowledge and in all judgment."[14] Here, in a few words, are the four pillars of the method of Christian ethics, in the order of the apostle's words: (1) a prayerful reliance upon God's grace; (2) the law of love as the norm; (3) knowledge of the facts, of the empirical situation in all its variety and relativity and particularity; and (4) judgment—i.e., decision—which is a matter of responsibility in humility.

This reference to humility, we might add, is no mere pretty moralism; it is the voice of grim realism. Our tragedy is that we often find ourselves in situations of ethical *inscrutabilia* and *imponderabilia,* like the destroyer commander in Monsarrat's novel *The Cruel Sea,* when he had to decide whether to drop a depth charge that would be sure to kill hundreds of desperate seamen struggling in the icy waters of the North Atlantic. He had a hope but no certainty that he would also destroy the U-boat on the sea floor, waiting there to destroy other ships and men in the convoy. As the C.O. said, there are times when all we can do is guess our best, and then get down on our knees and ask God's mercy. Monsarrat draws us a perfect picture of Luther's *pecca fortiter!*

ALLERGIC TO LAW

What we are doing here, if we were to express it in another theological key, the key of theological doctrine as distinguished from theological ethics, is to set a certain pattern and ordering of the four core categories of Freedom, Sin, Grace, and Law. A careful study of sundry Christian ethical systems will show that they may be char-

14 Phil. 1:9.

acterized or classified by the way in which they explicate or apply these four categories. Freedom, sin, grace, and law are related conceptually in quite identifiable fashion in Pauline, Augustinian, Thomist, Lutheran, Calvinist, and Arminian ethics, to cite some of the grand examples.

Hence, of course, as a Jesuit and a Thomist, Father Farraher says that the author of this book puts freedom first, and adds, "Of course, he applies it to excess."[15] The Dominican Urban Voll goes farther out by declaring that I have "what amounts to an allergy towards any kind of law."[16] Well, granted that "excess" and "allergy" are inexact terms, I am still willing meekly to accept what they say, and to rest content with Bishop Robinson's way of putting my case: "It is, of course, a highly dangerous ethic and the representatives of supernaturalistic legalism will, like the Pharisees, always fear it. Yet," he continues, "I believe it is the only ethic for 'man come of age.' To resist it in the name of religious sanctions will not stop it: it will only ensure that the form it takes will be anti-Christian."[17]

The focus of this "new morality" which is, as we have seen, not so new as many suppose, is clearly focused upon *decision*. In its retrospective function, looking back upon moral choices in the past, conscience makes *judgments;* it judges after the fact whether what was done was right or wrong, good or evil. In doing so, in this retrospective role, it works with all the advantages of hindsight. But in its prospective function, facing forward toward moral choices yet to be made, conscience makes *decisions;* it decides before the fact whether one path or another will be right or wrong, good or evil. Here it has no second-

[15] J. J. Farraher, S.J., "Notes on Moral Theology," *Theological Studies*, Vol. XVI (1955), p. 239.

[16] *The Thomist*, Vol. XVIII (1955), p. 94.

[17] *Honest to God*, p. 117.

guessing advantages; it is engaged in first-guessing, and much of its decision-making work entails a frightful measure of doubt and uncertainty and opacity. So much of the time we are making, at best, "educated guesses." Nevertheless, we have to decide, to choose whether we lean on law or ride out into the open for love's sake.

Life itself, in fact, is decision. Look at George Forrell's parable.[18] It is night, black dark. A man (you or I) is in a small boat, drifting down toward a roaring waterfall. He can hear, but he cannot see or be seen. He is wide-awake. Any choice he makes may be meaningless. If he rows, madly and no matter how hard, he may be swept over the edge. If he does nothing at all, he may be wedged safely against a rock until daylight and rescue come. He cannot know what to do. The current carries him along whatever he decides. It is impossible to ask for time out until he can pretest alternatives. And after all, not to choose either way is to choose one way. Not to make a decision is itself a decision. He cannot escape his freedom. He is bound to be free.

Existence not only demands decisions, it *is* decision. Staying alive demands a decision, and committing suicide demands a decision. He cannot escape freedom and therefore he cannot avoid decision. Nor can any of us. What the Christian situationist does is not to decide to decide; that is not an open election. His real election is to decide for love's sake, not law's sake.

THE CHRISTIAN REASON WHY

Acknowledging that every moral decision involves four factors (the ends, the means, the motives, and the foreseeable results both direct and indirect), then there appears to the Christian situationist to be nothing particu-

[18] *The Ethics of Decision* (Muhlenberg Press, 1955), pp. 3–5.

larly different or unique in a Christian's choices—except as to motive. *But even here* it is not true that the Christian's motive is unique because his "will" is "moved" by love. Lovingness is often the motive at work full force behind the decisions of non-Christian and nontheological, even atheist, decision makers. Christians have no monopoly of love, i.e., of the Holy Spirit, i.e., of the power of the love of God, i.e., of God himself. "Love Himself," said C. S. Lewis, "can work in those who know nothing of Him."[19] We have already noted God's worldly holiness and his uncovenanted grace for any man, as well as the point that God in his love of the world loves not an ideal man but man as he is, not an ideal world but the world as it is.

The Christian love ethic is, as Paul Lehmann says, a *"koinōnia* ethic" in the sense that the Christian's reason or motive of love and his understanding of its source is peculiar to his faith community.[20] But love itself is not peculiar to Christians! Many non-Christians "have" it and *do* it and "conduct" it, more fully than many Christians. There is no double goodness—one for among Christians, another for others. At the same time we are all struck by the matter-of-fact statement of a militant non-Christian, even anti-Christian, Bertrand Russell: "What the world needs is Christian love or compassion."[21]

What, then, is it that is special? The answer must be that what is special is that the Christian's love is a *responsive* love. Christian love is the love of gratitude, of thanksgiving to God for what he has done for us, for mankind, especially in the life, death, and resurrection of Jesus Christ. Christ's coming was not primarily to "make us

[19] *The Four Loves* (Harcourt, Brace and Company, 1960), p. 178.

[20] In *Christian Faith and Social Action,* ed. by J. A. Hutchison (Charles Scribner's Sons, 1953), pp. 102–114.

[21] *Human Society in Ethics and Politics,* p. viii.

good" but to give us faith in the goodness of God. The Christian ethic is peculiar because it is a *eucharistic* ethic, an ethic of thanksgiving. It comes from the compulsion to behave according to the belief of the Christian faith, Christian behaving according to Christian believing. It is different from any other ethos, not normatively but motivationally! The perennial problem of ethics is *akrasia,* the defect of the will, and Stephen Toulmin says of it, "Ethics finds the *reasons* for choosing the 'right' course: religion helps us to put our *hearts* into it."[22] Perhaps he knew of Hastings Rashdall's remark, "The chief good which the Christian lover will seek to realize for the loved is to make him also a lover."[23]

It is distinct from other moralities only because of its reason *for* righteousness, not by its standards *of* righteousness. It is not even distinguished by its monolithic law of love. No, what makes it different is a theological factor; the faith affirmation that God himself suffered for man's sake to reconcile the world in Christ. From this faith follows gratitude, a loving response to God's love, i.e., *agapē*. It is this eucharistic quality which is unique, nothing else.

Even if Christ were to be born a thousand times in a thousand stables, laid in a thousand mangers and in a thousand Bethlehems, unless he is born in our own hearts through our own responsive love, our gratitude responding to his redemptive love, we do not have the faith of the incarnation, we do not *know* what Christianity is.

But one more pinpointing is called for. It is not even exactly the gratitude that is unique. Men of many other faiths are grateful to God, and their gratitude can be the motive force of *their* decision-making too! There are other

[22] *Reason in Ethics* (Cambridge: Cambridge University Press, 1960), p. 219.

[23] *Conscience and Christ* (London: Gerald Duckworth & Co., Ltd., 1916), p. 126.

theological ethics which are, like our Christian ethics, powered by a eucharistic motivation. No, not even the gratitude is unique. What is precisely and exactly and starkly unique about the Christian ethic is *Christ*. It is a Christological ethic, not simply a theological ethic. When Bonhoeffer speaks of how Christ "takes form" among us here and now, this is his rather mystical but nonmetaphysical way of saying that every ethical imperative is contextual or situational, not propositional—but it is Christ who takes form with us when we conform to his commandment. Take away the doctrine of the incarnation and the Christian ethic is nothing special whatsoever.

In the Christian love ethic we do not seek to understand Christ in terms of love antecedently conceived; we understand love in terms of Jesus Christ.[24] This is the Christian faith ethic. The fact that the Christian ethic is theological gives it its species, but that it is Christological gives it its particularity. This is why in Christian ethics it is more than a doctrinaire formality to insist that before we ask the ethical question, "What shall I do?" comes the *pre*ethical question, "What has God done?" For this reason John Heuss once said that the key phrase in the Christian's activity is not "in order to" but "because of." Obedience to the love commandment is not a question of salvation but of *vocation*. Therefore, quoting a line of Thomas à Becket's in T. S. Eliot's play, *Murder in the Cathedral*, "The supreme treason is to do the right thing for the wrong reason."

The Question-Asking Way

George Bernard Shaw remarked somewhere that logic is interested in the reasons we give for things whereas ethics is interested in the things we give reasons for. The

[24] See John McIntyre, *On the Love of God* (Harper & Row, Publishers, Inc., 1962).

Christian ethic provides both sides, with its calculations of love and its loving calculations. And if we were to summarize what we have been saying in a single, simple formula, we should put it this way: "Christian ethics or moral theology is not a scheme of living according to a code but a continuous effort to relate love to a world of relativities through a casuistry obedient to love; its constant task is to work out the strategy and tactics of love, for Christ's sake."

Luther urged that the vocation of the Christian is to be a Christ to his neighbors. God does not need our service; we only serve God by serving our neighbors. And that is how we return his love. It is the only way we can return it. In the language of an American Lutheran, Joseph Sittler, "love is the function of faith horizontally just as prayer is the function of faith vertically."[25]

The modern history of the arts and sciences, and of the technologies that undergird them, makes it plain that they no longer bow down to nor cut their cloth to authoritarian principles. Their lifeline is no more handed down in advance or dropped from above by "revelation" or majesty. Men have turned to inductive and experimental methods of approach, working by trial and error, appealing to experience to validate their tentative and loosely held generalizations. As a strategy or method of inquiry and growth, it has worked with unprecedented success. Psychology, for example, got its start and growth this way. The same is true in many other sectors of the growing edge of the human enterprise. Now, at last, ethics and moral inquiry are doing it too. This is the new turn in the history of Christian ethics. This is the temper of clinical, case-centered, situational "concretion"—to use Bonhoeffer's word.

In a free society we have no official ethics any more than we have an official faith or political philosophy. But we

[25] *The Structure of Christian Ethics* (Louisiana University Press, 1958), p. 64.

can have a moral consensus. After all, it is not necessary to agree on an ethic to achieve living unity just as we need not hold a common epistemology or theory of knowledge to have an agreed body of scientific learning. Situation ethics is the most promising road to a moral community.

So, to make an end, let us say with John Dewey and James Tufts: "Of one thing we may be sure. If inquiries are to have any substantial basis, if they are not to be wholly up in the air, the theorist must take his departure from the problems which men actually meet in their own conduct. He may define and refine these; he may divide and systematize; he may abstract the problems from their concrete contexts in individual lives; he may classify them when he has detached them; but if he gets away from them he is talking about something which his own brain has invented, not about moral realities."[26]

[26] *Ethics* (Henry Holt & Company, 1908), p. 212.

X

An Appendix: Two Other Corruptions and Four Cases

Just to tidy things up before we close the covers on this essay, we should note that legalism is not the only travesty of Christian ethics giving it a bad image. There are two others, two other characteristic corruptions we ought at least to put into the record. Each could stand a book-length scrutiny itself. They are pietism and moralism, and like legalism, they distort what is good into what is bad. *Corruptio optimi pessima:* it is the corruption of the best which is worst.

PIETISM

These corruptions throw things out of focus. Pietism tends to corrupt religion by separating faith from society and daily life. Just as legalism is a distortion of legality, so pietism is a distortion of piety; legalism absolutizes and idolizes law, and pietism individualizes and subjectivizes piety. It reduces religion to religiosity by making it purely a personal and internal "spiritual" or mystical affair irrelevant to economic and political matters. It encourages the notion that religion ought not to "interfere" with politics or business, as if they were mutually exclusive spheres. It hates holy worldliness.

Pietism discards the Bible's prophetic combination of faith and action in favor of priestly softness and quietism, allowing a "social" side to religion only in a sect's or church's ingroup interests, in churchy affairs. It frowns upon all Christian involvement in questions of economic, racial, or political justice. It is always conservative, in fear of new forces, and often pours holy water on rightist extremism. One Philadelphia oil magnate has for years offered a major Protestant body huge sums of money on condition that its ministers would not "meddle" in secular affairs. Pietism, being what it is, gives aid and comfort to the secularization of culture and society by itself endorsing their divorce from faith, not only for the faithless (with whom the divorce makes sense) but even for the faithful.

To show what pietism is *not*, recall the rector of a congregation of West Indians in Miami who several years ago refused to surrender a list of Dade County members of the National Association for the Advancement of Colored People (NAACP), for whom he was secretary, because he knew perfectly well the state legislature's investigating committee was not engaged in sincere research to frame legislation. He knew they wanted to get the names of Negro "militants" and fire them from public service jobs in schools, welfare agencies, highway projects, and so on. The rector was willing to leave his parish and altar and pulpit untended and go to jail, agapeically, for the sake of love-justice in the civil rights struggle. (He was finally upheld by the courts, defended by a Negro attorney, Thurgood Marshall, who is now Solicitor General—so marches the cause!)

As Shaw said in his preface to *Androcles and the Lion,* the cry that religion ought not to "interfere" in politics and economics is always raised by those who do not want their power or their property threatened "by Jesus or any other reformers."

MORALISM

A second deadly distortion is moralism. Just as legalism absolutizes law and pietism individualizes piety, so moralism trivializes morality. It reduces ethics to pettifoggery or microethics, like the "microeconomics" John Galbraith described in *The Affluent Society*.[1] Moralism makes the moral life a matter of petty disciplines; it condemns smoking, dancing, playing cards, Sunday fun, drinking any alcoholic beverages, kissing and petting, missing church, having sinful thoughts, and the like, but never shows much concern for great issues of love and justice, never makes significant or daring demands upon men of goodwill. With this moral triviality often goes a kind of "works doctrine" in which the idea is that we are "saved" by being "good" and *can* be saved by following these petty, puritanical prohibitions.

Jesus' sarcastic remark about straining out the gnat and swallowing the camel fits moralism perfectly, as does his thrust at the Pharisaic opposition who paid tithes of mint and dill and cummin but ignored the weightier matters of justice, mercy, and faith (Matt. 23:23–24).

Yet another feature of moralism's triviality is that its ethic is an *easy* ethic as well as petty. By its radical reduction of the complexity and opacity of ethics to a code of moral minutiae, it cuts down "righteousness" to manageable size. Here again we have a reason for recalling Schweitzer's remark that an easy conscience is an invention of the devil.

America in the last two decades has seen an increase of religious activity and a decline of moral concern. Both the religion and the morals have been of a highly conventional or customary kind. When Father Drolet of the Roman Catholic Church and Mr. Foreman of The Methodist Church stood together in front of a picket line of their own people (who were trying to prevent integration of a New Orleans school), one holding aloft a crucifix and the other a Bible, to shame their people into going back to their homes, *nobody saw any connection between Christ, the Scriptures, and racial justice and loving-kindness.*

[1] (Houghton Mifflin Company, 1958), p. 104.

All the abstract or "in principle" preachments in the world will not get at the truth about us—whether we are or are not legalistic, pietistic, moralistic. Only concrete cases count. It is not ethics in general or ethical principles that truly assert anything meaningful; what does make meaningful assertions is *hyphenated* principles: "love *and*," love *and* situations. Love and a school integration; love and a subpoena; love and an abortion following incest by force and violence; love and a chance to get away with shoddy work; love and a hospital strike or a strike by doctors against medical social security legislation.

Here are four actual cases, no solutions included, to test our ethical method—exercises of a "sensitivity training" kind.

CHRISTIAN CLOAK AND DAGGER

I was reading Clinton Gardner's *Biblical Faith and Social Ethics*[2] on a shuttle plane to New York. Next to me sat a young woman of about twenty-eight or so, attractive and well turned out in expensive clothes of good taste. She showed some interest in my book, and I asked if she'd like to look at it. "No," she said, "I'd rather talk." What about? "Me." That was a surprise, and I knew it meant good-by to the reading I needed to get done. "I have a problem I can't get unconfused about. You might help me to decide," she explained. This was probably on the strength of what I was reading.

I learned that she had been educated in church-related schools, a first-rate college, and was now a buyer in women's shoes for a Washington store. We agreed, however, to remain mutually anonymous. Her problem? "O.K. This is it. One of our intelligence agencies wants me to be a kind of counterespionage agent, to lure an enemy spy into blackmail by using my sex." To test her Christian

[2] Harper & Brothers, 1960.

sophistication, I asked if she believed Paul's teaching about how our sex faculties are to be used, as in First Corinthians. Quickly she said, "Yes, if you mean that bit in the sixth chapter—your body is the temple of the Holy Spirit. *But,*" she added, "the trouble is that Paul also says, 'The powers that be are ordained of God.'"

The defense agency wanted her to take a secretary's job in a western European city, and under that cover "involve" a married man who was working for a rival power. Married men are as vulnerable to blackmail as homosexuals. They did not put strong pressure on her. When she protested that she couldn't put her personal integrity on the block, as sex for hire, they would only say: "We understand. It's like your brother risking his life or limb in Korea. We are sure this job can't be done any other way. It's bad if we have to turn to somebody less competent and discreet than you are."

So. We discussed it as a question of patriotic prostitution and personal integrity. In this case, how was she to balance loyalty and gratitude as an American citizen over against her ideal of sexual integrity?

SACRIFICIAL ADULTERY

As the Russian armies drove westward to meet the Americans and British at the Elbe, a Soviet patrol picked up a Mrs. Bergmeier foraging food for her three children. Unable even to get word to the children, and without any clear reason for it, she was taken off to a prison camp in the Ukraine. Her husband had been captured in the Bulge and taken to a POW camp in Wales.

When he was returned to Berlin, he spent weeks and weeks rounding up his children; two (Ilse, twelve, and Paul, ten) were found in a detention school run by the Russians, and the oldest, Hans, fifteen, was found hiding in a cellar near the Alexander Platz. Their mother's whereabouts remained a mystery, but they never stopped searching. She more than anything else was needed to reknit them as a family in that dire situation of hunger, chaos, and fear.

Meanwhile, in the Ukraine, Mrs. Bergmeier learned through a sympathetic commandant that her husband and family were trying to keep together and find her. But the rules allowed them to release her for only two reasons: (1) illness needing medical facilities beyond the camp's, in which case she would be sent to a Soviet hospital elsewhere, and (2) pregnancy, in which case she would be returned to Germany as a liability.

She turned things over in her mind and finally asked a friendly Volga German camp guard to impregnate her, which he did. Her condition being medically verified, she was sent back to Berlin and to her family. They welcomed her with open arms, even when she told them how she had managed it. When the child was born, they loved him more than all the rest, on the view that little Dietrich had done more for them than anybody.

When it was time for him to be christened, they took him to the pastor on a Sunday afternoon. After the ceremony they sent Dietrich home with the children and sat down in the pastor's study, to ask him whether they were right to feel as they did about Mrs. Bergmeier and Dietrich. Should they be grateful to the Volga German? Had Mrs. Bergmeier done a good and right thing?

"Himself Might His Quietus Make"

A staff doctor asked me to drop in on Jim. In his middle forties, married, five children, Jim had been in the hospital for more than a month, in a series of biopsies, X rays, blood tests, even exploratory surgery, to diagnose a breakdown in his digestive system.

He explained that a year or so earlier he'd started

having cramps after meals, went the "Tums route" with patent medicines of various kinds—nothing helped. A doctor said it might be an ulcer, but Jim was too busy for a GI series and kept at his work as construction engineer for a big builder of roads, bridges, and the like. We were just getting into things when the nurse arrived to ready him for some more tests. He thought they were to be final and would wrap it up one way or another. I left saying I'd be back again the next afternoon.

I found him in the solarium, looking very down and out. He thought we ought to go back to his room to talk, and when we got there he told me: "They say I have about three years, maybe less, that only a miracle can save me. They can only give me some stuff that will keep me alive a while. I can leave here tomorrow but can't do any work, just rest and take pills." After a pause he added: "The pills cost $40 about every three days. Who can afford that? They say if I stop them, then six months and I've had it."

We discussed it a bit and then he blurted out: "You know what is really bugging me? The company has me insured for $100,000, double indemnity. That's all the insurance I have. It's all I can leave Betts and the kids. If I take the pills and live past next October, then the policy will undoubtedly be canceled when it comes up for renewal. If I don't take them, at least my family will have some security. If I kill myself, they get even more. If I take the pills, borrow the money for them, and then the policy lapses, that will mean that they are going to be left penniless and in debt so that even the house goes. Over the hill, the poor house, and the kids farmed out. If I don't take the pills, I'm killing myself same as if I commit suicide with a razor or gas, seems to me." He closed his eyes.

"What would you do? How does it look to you? I want to do the right thing." We talked it over.

Special Bombing Mission No. 13

Early on August 6, 1945, the *Enola Gay* lifted off the airstrip on Tinian and a few hours later in broad daylight dropped a new weapon of mass extermination (they called it "Little Boy") on unsuspecting Hiroshima.[3] They had pretended to be on a routine weather mission, just as Powers did later in his famous U-2 over Sverdlovsk in 1960.

When the crew saw the explosion, they were silent. Captain Lewis uttered six words, "My God, what have we done?" Three days later another one fell on Nagasaki. About 152,000 were killed, many times more were wounded and burned, to die later. The next day Japan sued for peace.

Harry Truman had known nothing of the bomb until after his inauguration, following President Roosevelt's death. When Secretary Stimson told President Truman that "the most terrible weapon ever known" would soon be ready, he appointed an interim committee to consider how and when it should be used. They were all distinguished and responsible people on the committee. Most but not all of its military advisers favored using it. Winston Churchill joined them in favor. Top-level scientists said they could find no acceptable alternative to using it, but they were opposed by equally able scientists.

Admiral Leahy opposed its use altogether. Arthur Compton and E. O. Lawrence, among the nuclear physicists, wanted a warning demonstration first. So did Admiral Strauss. Assistant Secretary of War McCloy and Under Secretary of the Navy Bard agreed that the Japanese ought at least to be told what they were now faced with. On the other hand, intelligence experts said the Japanese

[3] F. Knebel and C. W. Bailey, "Hiroshima: The Decision that Changed the World," *Look,* June 7, 1960.

leaders were "blind to defeat" and would continue fighting
indefinitely, with millions of lives lost, unless something
like Little Boy shocked them into realism. Subsequently,
however, the U.S. Bombing Survey declared that the
Japanese "would have surrendered prior to November
first in any case."

In June the Interim Committee reported to the President, recommending that (1) the bomb be used against
Japan as soon as possible; (2) it should be used against
a dual target of military installations and civilian concentration; (3) it should be used without prior warning of
its coming or its nature. (One of the scientists changed his
mind, dissenting from the third point.)

A final discussion of these three issues in the report was
held in the White House, with President Truman present,
questioning but as yet undeclared. Also present were the
Secretary of War, vigorously defending the report as a
whole; the Assistant Secretary mainly opposed; General
Marshall was for it, Rear Admiral Strauss against it; Scientist Enrico Fermi was for it, Scientist Leo Szilard against
it. This meeting and discussion was *it*—now was the
"moment of truth," the moment of decision.

Index